'THEIR SKINS WERE DRY, THEIR LIPS BLACK AND CRACKED. THEY WERE ALL THIRSTY, WEARY, AND FOOTSORE. AND AMID THE VARIOUS CRIES ONE HEARD DISPUTES, REPROACHES, GROANS OF WEARINESS AND FATIGUE; THE VOICES OF MOST OF THEM WERE HOARSE AND WEAK. THROUGH IT ALL RAN A REFRAIN "WAY! WAY!
THE MARTIANS ARE COMING!"'

H.G. WELLS, *THE WAR OF THE WORLDS*
(HEINEMANN, LONDON, 1898)

ALIEN NATION

EDITED BY JOHN GILL, JENS HOFFMANN, GILANE TAWADROS

CONTENTS

PREFACE

Alien Nation is the culmination of a significant artistic, curatorial and institutional collaborative effort. This publication and the exhibition it accompanies are the result of the combined curatorial vision of the three co-curators: John Gill, Jens Hoffmann and Gilane Tawadros, who have each brought their unique perspectives on contemporary art practice to this project. Initially conceived when Gilane Tawadros was Director of inIVA and further developed by John Gill and Jens Hoffmann, *Alien Nation* has been realised thanks to their joint effort.

The ICA and inIVA are delighted to have given form to the project. We are organisations with our own specialisms, and this opportunity to work collaboratively has enabled us to combine our skills and resources in a new way. We hope the fruits of this collaboration will provide an enjoyable and thought-provoking experience for our audiences.

We extend our sincere gratitude to the 12 international artists exhibiting in *Alien Nation*. It is of course their works that are at the core of the project and their enthusiasm and commitment that have made it possible. With the generous support of the Esmée Fairbairn Foundation and Arts Council England, five artists have been commissioned to make new works for the exhibition and we are very pleased to present these works publicly for the first time. Our sincere thanks also go to the lenders who have generously parted with their works for the exhibition at the ICA and the duration of the exhibition tour.

The scale of current global insecurity and fear may feel unprecedented, but *Alien Nation* is a timely reminder that today's anxieties are in fact a frighteningly recurrent theme. In the Cold War narratives of the 1950s and '60s that were played out in science fiction films, fears surrounding a Communist invasion were displaced onto an alien, often racialised, 'other'. This exhibition and publication explore what could be considered another chapter in this all too real fiction, as today's fears about invasion or attack are frequently projected onto migrants, asylum seekers or people of Islamic faith. As is often the case in times of political unrest, it is the artists who point the way out.

EKOW ESHUN
ARTISTIC DIRECTOR, ICA

AUGUSTUS CASELY-HAYFORD
DIRECTOR, inIVA

'EVERYTHING LOOKED THE SAME BUT IT WASN'T. SOMETHING EVIL HAD TAKEN POSSESSION OF THE TOWN.'

DON SIEGEL, DIR. *INVASION OF THE BODY SNATCHERS*
(ALLIED ARTISTS, USA, 1956)

'WE ARE THE *MARTIANS...*'

BY GILANE TAWADROS AND JOHN GILL

In Kurt Vonnegut's book, *A Man Without a Country,* a memoir of life in George W. Bush's America, the writer confesses: 'I … feel that our country, for whose Constitution I fought in a just war, might as well have been invaded by Martians and body snatchers. Sometimes I wish it had been.'[1] Not exactly from another planet, Vonnegut's aliens chiefly take the form of right-wing journalists and politicians in the United States. The trope of the alien and the alien invasion is not a new one. Vonnegut himself first used the genre of science fiction in *Slaughterhouse Five* as a way to talk about the horrors of World War II and his experience of the bombing of Dresden. It recurs repeatedly in novels, films and artworks spanning a period of a hundred years from H.G. Wells' 19th-century novel *The War of the Worlds* (1898) to Ridley Scott's more recent film *Blade Runner* (1982). Articulating deep-seated fears about a rapidly changing world over which we exert little control, science fiction's narratives confront the apparent perils of the present seen through the prism of an imaginary future. Much has been written about the connection between science fiction cinema of the 1950s and 1960s and the Cold War, where fears of invasion, Communism and nuclear war were played out in fictional films that reflected contemporary anxieties. More recently, many artists have similarly used science fiction and the trope of the alien as a way of exploring the fear of difference and as a potent metaphor for the perceived threat of the outsider.

Alien Nation presents the work of 12 international artists all of whom explore themes of 'otherness' and 'difference' through the language and iconography of science fiction juxtaposed with original films and film posters from the 1950s and 1960s. The artworks encompass film, sculpture, photography, multimedia installation and painting – and expose a disturbing contemporary narrative in which the media perpetuate a terror of 'invasion' from immigrants, asylum seekers (indeed any racial, cultural or ethnic 'other') and position such 'outsiders' as the dominant threat to both family and national stability. Often witty and irreverent, these artists have adopted the figure of the extra-terrestrial and the alien(ated) landscape in order to comment upon the fantasies, fears and desires that lie, barely suppressed, beneath the surface of contemporary culture and society.

The storylines of 1950s and 1960s science fiction films were restricted, for the most part, to a small number of narratives that were played out over and over again in stories that rehearse the dangers of infiltration and attack by alien invaders. Scenarios often involve the 'invisible' duplication and transformation of friends, family and associates into emotionless aliens (*Invasion of the Body Snatchers*; *It Came from Outer Space*); the breeding of life-threatening alien life forms that threaten to overwhelm and wipe out human life (*Invasion of the Body Snatchers*; *The Thing from Another World*; *The Day of the Triffids*); the fear of annihilation (*The Day the Earth Stood Still*; *The War of the Worlds*; *Forbidden Planet*); the threat of brainwashing and mind control (*Village of the Damned*; *Quatermass and the Pit*); and anxieties about miscegenation and racial impurity (*The Day the Earth Stood Still*; *Village of the Damned*).

In the aftermath of 9/11 and the bombings in London and Madrid in recent years, these narratives have been re-played once again, this time in both documentary and fictional media representations, emerging from a society which has displaced its fears and paranoias onto the figure of the migrant, the asylum seeker and the Islamic 'other'. Images of the asylum seeker who poses a criminal threat to the wider society, or the terrorist whose outward appearance does not betray his/her loyalties to an 'alien' ideological cause; the brainwashing and 'radicalisation' of young men, converting them to militant Islam; and the fear of attack from long-range chemical weapons or terrorist devices closer to home, have become the subject of our collective nightmares, frequently stoked and fired up by politicians and the media so that it becomes almost impossible to distinguish reality from nightmare.

'NO REASON FOR ALARM': UFOS, COMMUNISM AND THE MEDIA

According to BBC radio news, reports were coming in from across the empire and from across the world of a massive unidentified flying object. Suspected at first of being a buzz bomb, the UFO was definitively identified on the US WMAL radio television broadcast as an alien spacecraft that had landed in Washington, DC at 3.47p.m. Eastern Standard Time. Government and Defence Department officials were concerned, however, about reports of panic in several large Eastern cities. 'I am authorised to assure you', said the news reporter, 'that so far there is no reasonable cause for alarm and that rumours of invading armies and mass destruction are based on hysteria and are absolutely false. I repeat these rumours are absolutely false'. Released in 1951, *The Day the Earth Stood Still* (directed by Robert Wise and based on a book, *Farewell to the Master,* by Harry Bates and a screenplay by Edmund H. North) was perhaps one of the most articulate of the science fiction film ripostes to the waves of fear and repression in the late 1940s and early 1950s which had culminated in the relentless anti-Communist campaign waged by the Republican senator from Wisconsin, Joseph R. McCarthy.

*Saturday Evening Post, c.*1948

The spacecraft in *The Day the Earth Stood Still* brings the peaceful alien Klaatu (played by actor Michael Rennie) to earth from a 'neighbouring' planet 250 million miles away to warn humankind of its impending doom: unless mankind ceases its experiments with new, more powerful weaponry with which it cannot be trusted, it will be destroyed by alien life forms who have successfully developed the means to curb violence and conflict. But the arrival of Klaatu (who subsequently assumes the Christian messianic alias 'Carpenter') provokes hysteria and violence, stoked by an omni-present media whose continuous commentary via radio and television broadcasts stirs up the populace's prejudices and fears of alien outsiders. 'You must be afraid', a journalist asks Klaatu/Carpenter, not realising that he is the alien whom the army is hunting down. 'I am afraid', replies Klaatu/Carpenter, 'when people replace reason with fear'.

In October 1938, Orson Welles' adaptation for radio of H.G. Wells' *The War of the Worlds* exploited the ubiquitous and authoritative voice of radio news coverage. Transferring H.G. Wells' story to the eastern seaboard of the contemporary United States, Orson Welles created the illusion of a real-time radio news broadcast which interrupted regular programming to bring listeners the news of a Martian invasion, provoking as a result wide-spread panic and hysteria amongst his radio audience. In the same year as Welles' broadcast, the House Un-American Activities Committee (HUAC) was established to protect the United States against Nazi penetration. Just as science fiction provided H.G. Wells with a vehicle for anticipating the epic conflict that came 14 years later with World War I, so Orson Welles' radio play was a harbinger of World War II. By the late 1940s, however, the threat of alien invasion had merged with a fear of sentiments and loyalties alien to the United States. As the Cold War froze relationships between the Soviet Union and the United States in the immediate post-war years, fears of Communism and Communist infiltration gripped America. In an effort to get to know and understand humankind, Klaatu/Carpenter in *The Day the Earth Stood Still* decides to live amongst ordinary Americans and goes to stay in a small boarding-house. Over breakfast (with the radio on in the background), one of his fellow boarders, Mrs Harley (Francis Bavier), looks up from her newspaper to contest the belief that this alien has come from another planet: 'If you want my opinion', she asserts, 'he comes from right here on earth and you know what I mean.' Klaatu was not an extra-terrestrial after all

News reporter, *The Day the Earth Stood Still*, 1951, film still

but rather an alien of an altogether different kind, although equally threatening to the American way of life.

A series of events had raised the temperature of fear and paranoia in the United States: the deepening of the Cold War and the Berlin crisis in June 1948; the victory of the Communists in China the following year; insecurity about American atomic monopoly (in September 1949, the Soviet Union exploded an atomic device a year earlier than American scientists had predicted); the confession in 1950 of the British scientist Dr Klaus Fuchs who admitted to having systematically turned over atomic secrets to the Soviets; the outbreak of the Korean War in 1950; and a series of spy scandals including the trial of Alger Hiss, a high-ranking State Department official found guilty of being a Soviet spy in the 1930s. These events set the scene for the passing of the Internal Security (or McCarran) Bill in September 1950 and the subsequent Communist witch hunts that stalked political and cultural life in the United States for several years. The Act 'required the registration of Communist and Communist-front organisations, forbade the employment of Communists in defense

plants, and barred anyone who had belonged to totalitarian organisations from entering the United States. An even more draconian provision authorized the establishment of concentration camps for Communists in times of national emergency'.[2] In the months and years leading up to the passing of the McCarran Bill, a tide of public opinion was turned to associate Communism with un-Americanism, clearing the way for the right-wing political backlash that was to follow.

It was not especially easy to link communism with un-Americanism and thus make it the issue in the country… . The keystone to the reformation of opinion was … the linking of all expressions of liberalism and radicalism to communism. Here the right wing relied upon Americans' characteristic nationalism. Communism was 'un-American' because it was atheistic, collectivistic, and international. This linking of Americanism to a highly specific set of values – organized religion, private property, and nationalism – made it un-American, hence Communistic, to be critical of, or to wish to change or challenge, those values and the institutions and policies which reflected them. Right-wing spokespeople hammered away

Gort, Klaatu and Helen on the spaceship ramp, *The Day the Earth Stood Still*, 1951, film still

at the theme that reformist activists and critics weakened America; they therefore had to be Communistic in identity or sympathy, and, in the national interest, had to be exposed and quarantined. [3]

Although President Truman had vetoed the McCarran Bill on the grounds that it infringed civil liberties, his consistently anti-Communist foreign policy was echoed by the State Department's attitude towards the American film industry. Inquiring about 'American Motion Pictures in the Post-War World', the Department stated its desire to 'co-operate fully in the protection of American motion pictures abroad', in return for the industry's co-operation in 'insuring that the pictures distributed abroad will reflect credit on the good name and reputation of this country and its institutions.' Two years later, on 21 September 1947, the House Un-American Activities Committee (HUAC) issued subpoenas to 43 members of the Hollywood film industry requiring that they appear as witnesses before the Committee during its October hearings in Washington. The subsequent prosecution and imprisonment of the 'Hollywood Ten' as they became known was only a foretaste of what was to come three years later when the HUAC returned to Hollywood with devastating results. In its Annual Report for 1953, the Committee reported on the successful outcome of its witch hunts in the film industry between 1951 and 1953: 'it can be stated on considerable authority that perhaps no major industry in the world today employs fewer members of the Communist Party than does the motion-picture industry.' [4]

The media were an abiding presence during the Communist witch hunts of the McCarthy era, bringing 'live' coverage into the homes of ordinary Americans as John Frankenheimer brilliantly portrayed in his 1962 film *The Manchurian Candidate,* in which the figure of Senator John Iselin (James Gregory) is a thinly disguised Senator Joe McCarthy. In one scene where Iselin launches an attack on card-carrying Communists in the Defense Department on the floor of the Senate, the action is refracted through a television screen that disseminates the events happening in the background. Set during and immediately after the Korean War, *The Manchurian Candidate* revolves around the brainwashing by Communists of a US

Senator Iselin, *The Manchurian Candidate*, 1962, film still

soldier, Staff Sergeant Raymond Shaw (Laurence Harvey), who is programmed to become a robotic assassin. Back home, having been awarded the Congressional Medal of Honour, Shaw is 'activated' into killing by his American operator (who turns out to be his Communist-baiting mother and wife of Senator Iselin, played by Angela Lansbury). 'I served them. I fought for them. I'm on the point of winning for them the greatest foothold they will ever have in this country', says Lansbury. 'They paid me back by taking your soul away from you.'

Representatives of the media – whether radio or television broadcasters or newspaper journalists – are commentators in many 1950s science fiction movies. *The Day the Earth Stood Still* opens with radio news broadcasts from around the world and journalists provide a running commentary to events as they unfold throughout the film, even interviewing Klaatu/Carpenter at one point. In *The Thing from Another World* (1951), the journalist Scotty (Douglas Spencer) is waiting for a story and invokes the US Constitution when he thinks he may be prevented from covering the discovery of a spaceship and its inhabitants: 'This is the biggest story since the parting of the Red Sea.' At the end of the film, it is Scotty who issues the paranoid warning: 'Watch the skies everywhere … keep looking … keep watching the skies.'

Welles' radio broadcast uses the conceit of interrupting a number of times a performance by Ramon Racello and his orchestra in the aptly-named Meridien Room of the Park Plaza in New York City, to bring his listeners news updates of the alien invasion on the West Coast of America. Two decades earlier, prior to World War II and at the height of American isolationist sentiment, the United States had been cut off from developments beyond its borders. World War II had changed all that. Newspapers and radio broadcasts became an important conduit for news beyond America's shores and a wider world. Media coverage lent further authenticity to science fiction stories that frequently relied on its depiction of ordinary, everyday America taken over and transformed by creatures from another planet.

ROBOTS AND ALIENS: THE GOOD, THE BAD AND THE UGLY

The aliens and robots that populate science fiction films of the 1950s are an assortment of the good, the bad and the ugly. The Frankenstein-like 'Thing' (James Arness) in *The Thing from Another World*

Atom-Anxious America

by ROLAND WILD

Children in a Los Angeles school take cover in a civil defence drill, *Illustrated*, 3 March 1951

Long Island H-bomb shelter, *Illustrated*, 9 July 1955

United States marines watch a test explosion of an American atom bomb at Yucca Flats, Nevada, *c*.1950

er Hiss, accused by **Whittaker Chambers** of giving secret Government documents to the Com-
aists, denied the charges and was convicted of perjury. Here he smiles with his wife after trial

UNITED PRESS

The CIA gets some of its best information from ex-Reds—like Mrs. Vladimir Petrov, shown being
hustled to a plane in Australia by Russian guards. Later, she was rescued and granted political asylum.

VE LEFT: From 'What Made Them Turn Red?', *Look*, 5 August 1950
VE RIGHT: *Saturday Evening Post*, 30 October 1954
OW: Senator Joseph R. McCarthy attending Senate labour hearings, February 1957

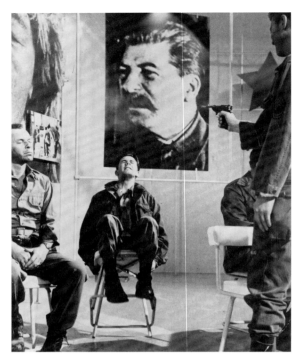

Brainwashing of American Staff Sergeant Raymond Shaw by Communists, *The Manchurian Candidate*, 1962, film still

is closer to the monsters dreamt up by Mary Shelley's 19th-century gothic imagination than any futuristic, advanced life form; while Klaatu's human appearance in *The Day the Earth Stood Still* belies his super-human capacity to resist disease and ageing. Other aliens are more distant from human form.

The aliens in *It Came from Outer Space* (1953) are forced to take on human appearance while they repair their damaged spaceship because their true alien form is too hideous and terrifying for human beings to behold and, by implication, to accept. These are peaceful aliens who simply want to be left alone to fix their ship and return home but they are well aware (as Klaatu is) of man's instinctively violent response not only to those who are different but also to their own race. The robot Gort (Lock Martin), who eventually descends from the spaceship in *The Day the Earth Stood Still* (after soldiers have shot at Klaatu having mistaken his gift for a weapon), is a massive metallic humanoid figure from a race of intergalactic policemen whose job it is to enforce peace and avert violence and conflict in the rest of the universe. Gort's immense destructive powers are triggered by the assaults on Klaatu in the same way that the visit to earth by these alien/robot visitors has been provoked by the threat of mankind's military expansionism.

In *Forbidden Planet* (1956), the sophisticated robot Robby has been programmed by his creator, the scientist Dr Morbius (a space-age Prospero played by actor Walter Pidgeon), in such a way as to make it impossible for him to kill or destroy human life. The mysterious and invisible alien life form that inhabits the planet Altair 4 and destroys the lives of innocent crew members turns out at the end of the film to be not an alien life form but rather the 'monstrous Id' of the scientist Dr Morbius, a horrific alter-ego that acts out his murderous and suppressed desires. Like *Quatermass*, which originated as a television series on BBC in 1953, *Forbidden Planet* presented as the greatest threat to mankind its inner destructive nature rather than any extra-terrestrial bent on the annihilation of the earth. As the scientist Quatermass pronounces at the conclusion of the television version of *Quatermass and the Pit* (1958–59): 'Every war, crisis, witch-hunt, race riot and purge, is a reminder and warning. We are the Martians. If we cannot control the inheritance within us, this will be the second dead planet.'

Aliens and robots feature in the works of many of the artists in the *Alien Nation* exhibition, although what is striking is how ambiguous and indeterminate these characters of contemporary art are both in appearance and morality. A reflection of the more equivocal times in which we live and

Robby, *Forbidden Planet*, 1956, film still

also of the more open-ended structure of contemporary art by comparison with film narrative (which has a beginning, middle and end, and moves invariably towards a resolution of some kind), there are no clear-cut goodies and baddies, no positively good aliens or downright evil ones. **Laylah Ali**'s bizarre humanoid figures are indeterminate beings that look alternately like children in extravagant dressing-up costumes or freakish genetic mutations, part-animal and part-human. In earlier works populated by Ali's 'Greenheads' and 'Blueheads', the physical indeterminacy of the figures – alien/human, male/female, black/white – reflected their ambiguous morality. In one work, Greenheads wearing white surgical masks lift up small babies for inspection. It is impossible to discern whether their actions are murderous or humane, and the artist herself offers no comforting answers or explanations but rather leaves them, as she puts it, 'to act as a question mark'.[5] In these recent colour drawings, the identities of Ali's creations are obscured by masks, balaclavas and head-dresses. Some are malformed, either lacking limbs or with additional protruding limbs and growths that sprout from their hips and heads. One creature enveloped in fabric appears gagged and strait-jacketed. Another goggle-eyed alien wears an elaborate feather head-dress: a peculiar flightless animal that is part-human and part-bird. These strange creatures might be figments of a surreal imagination or discarded mutations of some terrible scientific experiment.

The source for **Hamad Butt**'s early video work *The Triffid* (part II of the *Transmission* installation) made in 1990 was a drawing of a triffid on an early Penguin edition of John Wyndham's *The Day of the Triffids*, first published in 1951. Possibly the 'outcome of a series of ingenious biological meddlings'[6] and cultivated on an industrial scale in order to extract its valuable oil, the triffids were tall, large-rooted plants whose venomous sting could blind its victims and feed on their decomposing human flesh. When the majority of people on earth are blinded as a result of witnessing an extraordinary comet display, the triffids are in a position to take over the planet. For Butt, the triffid was a metaphor for a contemporary and equally deadly epidemic that was capable of generating as much fear as Wyndham's toxic, walking plants. He was interested in exploring what he described as the 'apprehension of the Triffids of the day' and the response to its present-day equivalent.

To remain protected from the danger of the Triffids might mean life on human reservations, a sort of reversal of the usual contaminated concentration camp. We have suspicions of scientific meddling that erupts with blindness to the threats of the origins of the accompanying plague. The Triffids blind their victims, the 'comet' blinds the populace, light in excess blinds the viewer, 'what bursts in the bewilderment of the summit, moreover, as soon as life begins to go astray. The need for an attraction – the necessity, found in the autonomy of human beings, of imposing one's value upon the universe – introduces from the outset a disordered state in all of life'.[7]

Cover of John Wyndham's *The Day of the Triffids*, Penguin, first edition, 1954

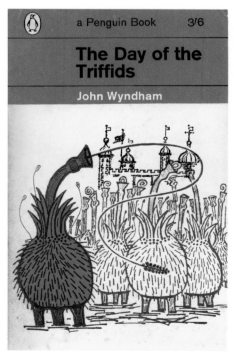

Butt's video isolates the outline of the triffid and animates it through a spectrum of shifting colours, electrifying and magnifying its movements. Seen like this, the triffid mutates into an object of beauty as well as an object of fear. The triffid embodied many of Butt's preoccupations as an artist – the intersection of art and science, the arcane (alchemy) and the popular (science fiction), sexuality and death. These themes permeate Butt's works, invoking the precariousness of human existence and the settled sense of security which is shattered so abruptly by the coming of the triffids in Wyndham's fiction and by AIDS in the contemporary world.

H.G. WELLS' THE WAR

Produced by GEORGE PAL
WHO GAVE YOU
'DESTINATION MOON'& 'WHEN WORLDS COLLIDE'
DIRECTED BY   SCREENPLAY BY
BYRON HASKIN · BARRE LYNDON
BASED ON THE NOVEL BY H.G.WELLS
A PARAMOUNT PICTURE
DISTRIBUTED BY PARAMOUNT FILM SERVICE LTD.

The War of the Worlds, 1953, original British film poster

WORLDS
Color by Technicolor
Cert X
A MIGHTY PANORAMA OF EARTH-SHAKING FURY !

On the cover of the book (of the film, of the television programme) an image of the creature that is not anything as distant as the castrated male genitalia, yet it creeps closer to that dreaded desire as it takes the power of mobilization to itself. And we see the ejaculating approach of blindness, there is the deflation of the 'phallic gaze' with the castration of the 'father-less' which is to say the leader-less masses. Thus they lend themselves to the rule of fear that is generated by pudenda.[8]

In most of the science fiction narratives of the 1950s, the tension arises from the fear of the apocalypse that is yet to happen and the action takes place on the brink of this apocalyptic event. *The Day of the Triffids*, written at the height of the Cold War, imagines the aftermath of the apocalypse in a post-war world where the complete annihilation of the human race was seen as a distinct possibility. As Michael Beadley tells the sighted survivors in *Triffids:* 'From 6 August 1945, the margin of survival has narrowed appallingly. Indeed, two days ago it was narrower than it is at this moment… . In any single moment of the years since then the fatal slip might have been made. It is a miracle that it was not'.[9]

In the world of **David Huffman**'s paintings, the trauma has already taken place many years earlier. Huffman creates an alternative universe that still bears the trauma of the past and present, carrying it forward into the future. In earlier paintings, from the late 1990s, Huffman conceived the Traumasmiles: black-faced minstrels that wear a perpetual grin, fixed in place permanently by the trauma of slavery and its repercussions through time. As Huffman explains, 'trauma was the subverted awareness of the trauma of slavery itself – the horrific holocaust that wasn't digested or dealt with in a mature way. So to me it was very traumatic to create characters with big smiles when that had actually occurred for so long. The smile was false, not a simple expression of joy or happiness, but a disguise that covered an internal anguish. Pain was subverted through that smiling face'.[10]

Alongside the race of Traumasmiles are their powerful robotic creations, the Traumabots, which are animated and powered by the Traumasmiles 'who get inside and become physically connected to them … it is a neurological connection in that they can feel everything that happens to the robots.

David Huffman, *Steppin' Stone*, 2006, mixed media on paper, 97 x 127 cm, Courtesy the artist and Patricia Sweetow Gallery, San Francisco

They become one.'[11] In a reversal of the classic science fiction storyline where aliens occupy the bodies of human beings, here the Traumabots are inhabited by the Traumasmiles, endowing them with both a body and power. For Huffman, who grew up in the United States on a diet of television programmes like *Astroboy*, *Shogun Warriors*, *Transformers* and *Star Trek*, science fiction provided both intellectual and aesthetic source material whose storylines frequently dealt with the fear of difference: 'I've always been interested in the way '50s science fiction came out of McCarthyism and the idea that the Reds are here. The whole alien and UFO thing was mostly about other people, other cultures.'[12] In *It's All Over Now, Baby Blue* (2006) – Huffman's new three-panel screen work – the artist creates a world where extra-terrestrial protagonists collide with recent events. References to conflicts (from Vietnam to Iraq), in which indigenous populations are overpowered by military might, are intermingled in Huffman's narrative paintings with references to the science fiction movie *Beneath the Planet of the Apes*, with its inverted evolutionary narrative in which apes evolve from humans: 'the Traumasmiles are shaped by contemporary socio-political minefields that are played out in my parallel universe of Traumanauts'.

Outer space provides an other-worldly place where earthly conflicts and tensions can be resolved and where new alliances can be forged. The crew of the Starship Enterprise in *Star Trek* (first aired in the early 1960s at the height of the Civil Rights Movement) presented an idealised interplanetary and ethnic alliance. The first interracial kiss on television, between Captain Kirk (William Shatner) and Lieutenant Uhura (Nichelle Nichols, whose character's name was inspired by *uhuru*, the Swahili word for freedom) in the 1968 episode 'Plato's Children', played out mixed race relationships in the furthest reaches of the universe, that were still capable of inflaming violent racist passions and reprisals on our own planet.

Mario Ybarra Jr.'s mural, *Brown and Proud* (2006), imagines a very different alliance between rebels not only from different spaces/places but also from different planets. Ybarra, who himself combines a variety of roles including artist, educator, gallerist, social anthropologist and archivist, creates artworks and interventions that frequently involve constructing a platform for the meeting of different worlds that blend and cross-pollinate in contemporary Chicano art culture: North American/Mexican; popular culture/Hollywood; science fiction/political reality. In this new work, Ybarra pictures a meeting between the hairy alien rebel Chewbacca (a giant fur-covered Wookie) and the Mexican revolutionary Zapata, both rebels engaged in battling against an awesome empire, whether galactic or earthly. In Ybarra's universe, the partnership between Chewbacca and Zapata also represents the coalition of political revolt and popular culture as a strategy for resistance against more conventional (and potentially alienating) political structures.

A different kind of displacement occurs in **Yinka Shonibare**'s *Dysfunctional Family* (1999). A typical family group – mother, father and two kids – Shonibare's nuclear family are remarkable only in the sense that they obviously belong to another species from another planet and, perhaps, even from another universe. With their short bodies and disproportionately large heads, Shonibare's *Dysfunctional Family* is a witty and acerbic play on the fear of difference. Based on popular images of aliens, Shonibare's extra-terrestrials are fashioned out of the batik cloth that has become the signature of many of the artist's works with its indeterminate status (Indonesian fabric exported to Africa that has come to be seen as traditional African fabric). This alien family is equally indeterminate. Conventional in every respect, other than its questionable outer space origin, Shonibare's *Dysfunctional Family* is a playful spin on the legal and social designation of the 'alien' as a marker of difference and the fears and fantasies that it ignites.

The term 'alien' was still being employed by the British government as late as 1970 to designate foreigners entering the country who were also obliged to register their presence at a police station. The Alien Act of 1793 had been enacted in Britain after the French Revolution had turned to terror and was designed to monitor and register all foreigners entering Britain, the information being sent to a central index at the Home Office. By 1800 the Alien Office had become 'the centre of Britain's spy network, watching subversives through the apprehending and copying of letters sent through the Post Office'.[13] Fifteen years later, the Federalists in the United States passed the Alien and Seditions Acts (1798) as a response to the recent influx of political refugees – French Jacobins, Irish rebels, English and Welsh radicals – who had become outspoken supporters of the Republican party.[14] To some radical screenwriters in the United States in

the late 1940s, the mounting anti-Communist crusade bore a striking resemblance to the events that had taken place 150 years earlier. As the writer Philip Dunne wrote: 'Attempts to force conformity of opinion are nothing new in the United States. The Alien and Seditions Act of the first Adams administration, directed against the Jeffersonians who were thought to be too sympathetic to the French revolutionaries, afford what is almost a direct parallel to the anti-Communist proposals of today.' [15]

Alongside Shonibare's *Dysfunctional Family*, the floor of the gallery space is littered with strange metallic objects that could be extra-terrestrial constructions or exquisite space debris, reclaimed as ornamental sculptures or over-sized Christmas decorations. There is a kind of alchemy to the practice of the artist **Marepe** whose works frequently transform found, everyday objects into poetic and evocative artworks that invite both physical and social interactions. In earlier installations such as *The Itinerant Merchants* (1996) or *Cafezinho Pushcart* (1996), Marepe reproduces or else imports into the gallery space the mobile carts, suitcases

and tables used by street vendors in the markets of Salvador da Bahia in Brazil; or, as in *Embutido Renconcavo-Renconcavo embutido* (2003), reconstructs the simple, wooden dwellings of Bahia's poorer inhabitants in the contemporary art space. The process by which Marepe replicates and transforms the everyday into something that merits our care and attention is echoed in countless science fiction narratives in which the familiar and commonplace are disrupted or suspended by the arrival of aliens in our domestic landscape.

ALIEN LANDSCAPES:
DESERTS, CITIES AND SUBURBIA

No-one would have believed, in the last years of the nineteenth century, that this world was being watched keenly and closely by intelligences greater than man's and yet as mortal as his own; that as men busied themselves about their various concerns they were scrutinized and studied, perhaps almost as narrowly as a man with a microscope might scrutinize the transient creatures that swarm and multiply in a drop of water. With infinite complacency men went to and fro over this globe about their little affairs, serene in their assurance of their empire over matter.[16]

Alien spaceships can land just about anywhere: the Arizona desert, Antarctica, small-town America, Washington, DC. New Jersey is the site of the Martian invasion in the Mercury Theatre's 1938 production of Wells' *The War of the Worlds*. Sand Rock, Arizona is the setting for the 1953 movie *It Came from Outer Space*. The empty, uninhabited desert plains that stretch for miles around the small community of Sand Rock are reminiscent of the site where the testing of the atom bomb took place in the 1940s. Amateur astronomer John Putnam (Richard Carlson) has abandoned city living to relocate to Arizona and is watching the night sky through his telescope when he sees a spacecraft crash land in the desert. The spaceship has been damaged in its collision with the ground and needs urgent repair. The aliens then kidnap some of Sand Rock's inhabitants and assume their physical appearance so that they can go about their repairs undisturbed. Driving through the desert, Putnam and his fiancée Ellen (Barbara Rush) come across Frank and George (Joe Sawyer and Russell Johnson), two of the town's residents (significantly, their work

involves repairing the telegraph / telephone communication lines) behaving strangely, very unlike their true selves. It is here that the aliens reveal what they are doing: 'Don't be afraid. It is within our power to look like you or anyone. For a time it will be necessary to do this'.

This is the moment that artists **Ellen Gallagher** and **Edgar Cleijne** elect to rework in one of the five 16mm projections that make up the film installation *Murmur* (2003–04). Scratching directly into the film emulsion, the artists create a parallel narrative that moves along and hijacks the already existing one. Set in the desert, a sheriff's office, an empty stretch of road at night, *Monster* takes place in elastic in-between space, where the aliens – the others – all appear monstrously white with blond hair and sightless eyes that could not so easily 'pass' as human. While deep space offers alien life forms that can replicate human likeness, the deep sea is home to bizarre and unfamiliar species that skulk in the depths of the ocean. These antediluvian life forms are the inspiration for Gallagher's series of drawings *Watery Ecstatic* (2001– ongoing), which subsequently gave rise to the stop action film of the same name that also forms part of the

Putnam confronts aliens in the guise of Frank and George, *It Came from Outer Space*, 1953, film still

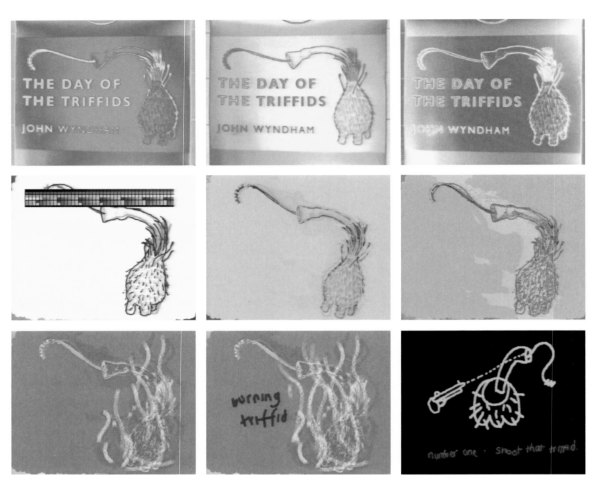

Hamad Butt, *The Triffid* (part II of the *Transmission* installation), 1990
Film stills from U-matic video transferred to DVD, 17 minutes, 8 seconds, Courtesy Ahmad Butt, London

Murmur installation. In *Blizzard of White*, a 'shoal of spiky white plasticine creatures … sink slowly toward the ocean floor against an inky graphite backdrop of underwater volcanoes';[17] while *Kabuki* features a 3-D animation of a fractal, fragmented 'wiglady' slowly looping down into the ocean's unfathomable depths.

As the first thing one encounters when entering the space, *Suberboo* is both the coda and opening 'credit' of an installation that is thought through as a film. Constructed of already existing signs and data, *Suberboo* takes a drawing from Gallagher's *Ebony* series as a ground. In this animation the camera moves along the drawing to create a fight sequence with Bruce Lee and Jim Kelly. Adding to the layering of images and references that *Murmur* combines, the soundtrack is extracted from a Dizzee Rascal sample of Javanese gamelon music. *Murmur* sets the tone for a journey that gives history, myths, autobiographies and fictions a form that the artists describe as follows: 'The

physical form of *Murmur* is a singular entity made up of several parts that, taken together, have the properties of expressive phrasing. The various forms within *Murmur* are modulated to create emphasis. This applies to *Murmur* as a whole as well as to the way forms are combined within the individual 16mm projections that make up *Murmur*.'

It is small-town America that is conjured up by **Kori Newkirk**'s beaded landscapes. Newkirk's images of suburban America are constructed from beaded curtains that visualise fragments of small town America that you might see speeding along a US highway: a telegraph pole (*Echo*, 2001) or one-storey houses viewed from a distance (*The World and the Way Things Are*, 2001). Newkirk's works quite literally fracture these icons of everyday American life, breaking up its seamless appearance. The world envisaged by Newkirk recalls the small Californian town of Santa Mira, the setting for Don Siegel's *Invasion of the Body Snatchers* (1956), which is irrevocably changed by the alien invasion that engulfs it. Nothing seems the same when Dr Miles Bennell (Kevin McCarthy) and his girlfriend Becky (Dana Wynter) return to Santa Mira: 'Everything looked the same but it wasn't. Something evil had taken possession of the town.' According to the local psychiatrist Dan Kauffman, 'an epidemic of mass hysteria' had taken over Santa Mira. Huge seed-pods are deposited at the homes of Santa Mira's residents, eventually bursting open to reveal the exact likenesses of their hosts. From the town centre, trucks are loaded up with pods to travel out through the whole country like 'a malignant disease'. The alien replicants hold out the promise of an untroubled, simple world where everyone is the same and where desire, ambition and faith have been eradicated. The film's penultimate scene pictures Bennell escaping from Santa Mira and trying desperately to get the attention of truck and car drivers on the freeway as trucks roll out of Santa Mira, loaded with hundreds of giant, alien pods: 'Listen to me… We're in danger… Help! Help! We're in danger. Listen to me. You fools, you're in danger. Listen to me. They're after you. They're after all of us. They're here already…'.

Henna Nadeem's exquisite collages, saturated in colour, picture the serene, idyllic English countryside through a lens of abstract patterns that obscure the landscape. The source material for her digitally-manipulated images are photographs of Britain, originally published by *Country Life* magazine from the 1930s to the 1970s in a series of popular publications entitled *The Picture Books of Britain*, which from 1957 turned to super-real colour reproduction. Overlain with elaborate, abstract designs, the familiar English landscape appears alien and strange, almost as if it were being seen for the first time by extra-terrestrial visitors. Just as in *It Came from Outer Space*, where we see the planet from the perspective of the one-eyed, stout bubble-shaped creatures that arrive from another world, Nadeem's photographs present us with a familiar landscape that has been irreversibly altered.

Hew Locke's installation is fabricated from familiar objects and broken toys that have been assembled and re-configured by the artist to create a strange fleet of shimmering gold and silver vessels that invades the gallery space. It is difficult to work out the origins of this arresting but eerie flotilla. Locke's assemblage appears as a contemporary re-working of a baroque altarpiece, populated by gun-toting, menacing anatomical dolls. With their gold and silver swords and shields, their guns and bullet belts, Locke's sinister cherubs have lost all trace of innocence and offer up a dystopian vision of the future − conjured up from the past and the present − with its hints of colonial invasion and indiscriminate violence. For Locke, science fiction works in parallel to his own creative practice, opening up 'a doorway into a different reality … that speaks to this reality'.[18]

Like Nadeem and Locke, many of the artists in *Alien Nation* envision a world in which the familiar has been rendered strange, or vice versa, with the alien depicted as ordinary and everyday. The fears and paranoias that might have been projected onto an apocalyptic future or onto aliens from elsewhere have been accommodated into the present whose trajectory remains equivocal and open-ended. Perhaps, after all, the future has arrived and the aliens are already here.

NOTES

1. Kurt Vonnegut, *A Man without a Country*, London: Bloomsbury, 2006, pp 98−99.
2. Maldwyn A. Jones, *The Limits of Liberty: American History 1607−1992*, Oxford and New York: Oxford University Press, 1995, p.530.
3. Larry Ceplair and Steven Englund, *The Inquisition in Hollywood: Politics in the Film Community, 1930−60*, Urbana and Chicago: University of Illinois Press, 2003, pp 202−03.
4. ibid., p.361.
5. Rebecca Walker, 'Interview', in Jessica Morgan, Rebecca Walker and Susan Wise, *Laylah Ali*, Boston: ICA, 2001, p.23.
6. John Wyndham, *The Day of the Triffids*, London: Penguin, 2000, p.18.
7. Hamad Butt in *Hamad Butt: Familiars*, London: Institute of International Visual Arts in association with John Hansard Gallery, 1996, p.50.
8. ibid., pp 50−51.
9. John Wyndham, op. cit., p.96.
10. Interview with Patricia Sweetow, 30 May 1999.
11. ibid.
12. David Huffman, quoted by Kenneth Baker in the *San Francisco Chronicle*, 5 September 2001.
13. Clive Bloom, *Violent London: 2,000 Years of Riots, Rebels and Revolts*, London: Pan Books, 2004, p.183.
14. Maldwyn A. Jones, op. cit., p.87.
15. Ceplair and Englund, op. cit., p.245.
16. H.G. Wells, *The War of the Worlds* (1898), republished in London by Penguin Books, 2005, p.7.
17. Caoimhín Mac Giolla Léith in *Ellen Gallagher: Orbus*, Edinburgh: Fruitmarket Gallery, and Zürich: Hauser & Wirth, 2005
18. Hew Locke interviewed by Jens Hoffmann and quoted in Jens Hoffmann, 'The Truth is Out There' in this publication.

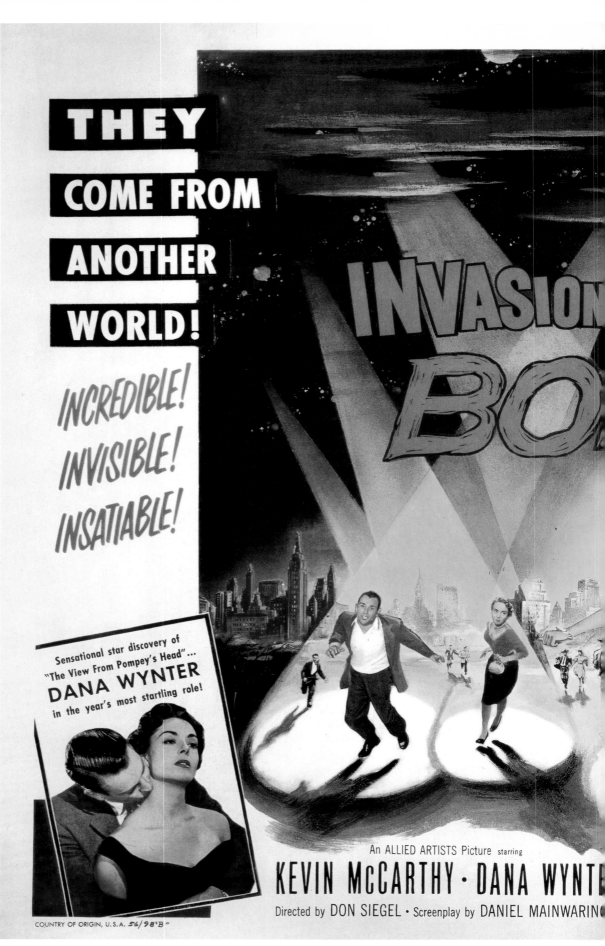

Invasion of the Body Snatchers, 1956, original US film poster

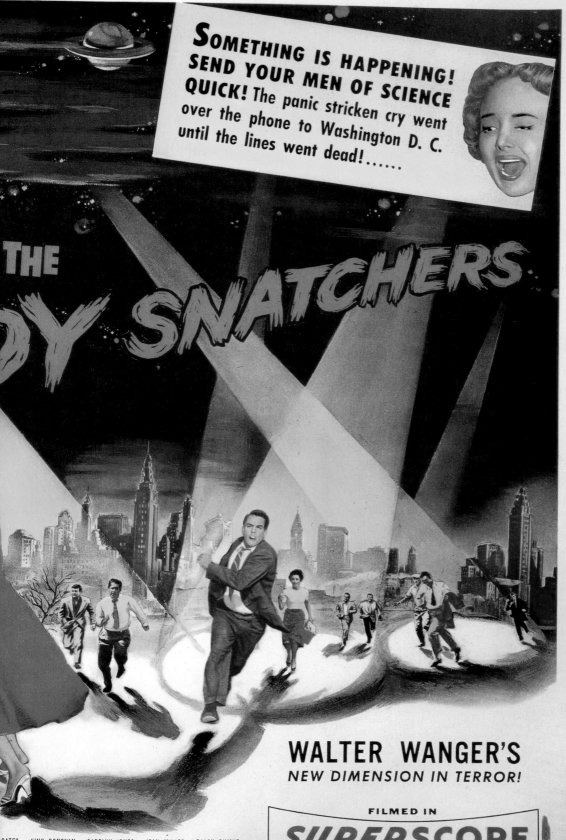

'WE COME IN PEACE!
WE COME IN PEACE!'

MARTIAN AMBASSADOR,
TIM BURTON, DIR. *MARS ATTACKS!*
(WARNER BROS PICTURES, USA, 1996)

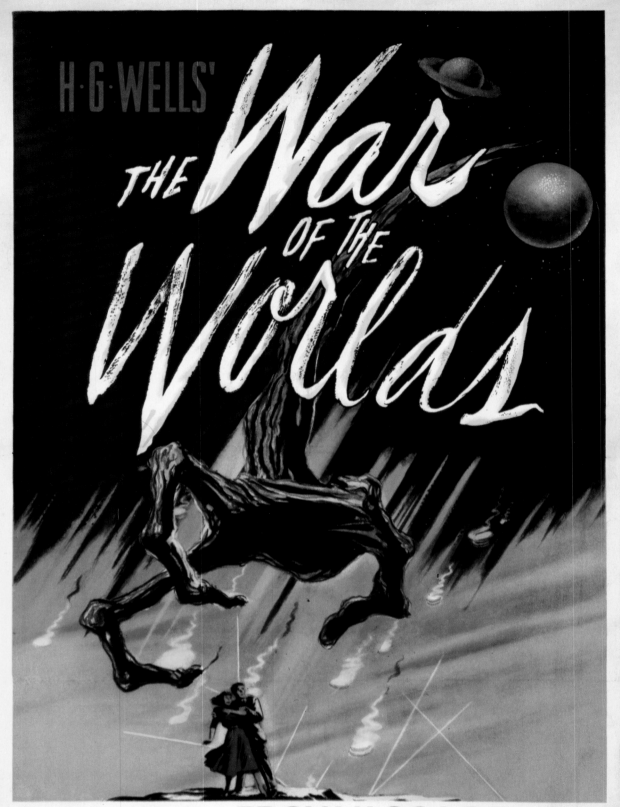

THE *TRUTH* IS *OUT THERE*

BY JENS HOFFMANN

TRUST ME ... the world is full of people who believe in alien abductions, extra-terrestrial conspiracies and Martians invading our planet, and quite often these are the same people who believe that immigrants are privileged in our society, and that minorities have too much power. What is articulated through such convictions is the fear and paranoia of the unknown and the unfamiliar that culminates in a collective psychosis about a secret plot to take over the world, whether by aliens, immigrants or other outcasts and strangers. Interestingly enough, the notion of the alien and immigrant has often been connected and even more often confused. In the world of science, an alien is a life form that exists and originates outside our planet, which is so far the only planet that allows for life from a biological perspective. The concept of aliens is therefore completely imaginary: no one has ever seen an extra-terrestrial. In legal terms, an alien is a person who is not a native or naturalised citizen of the land in which she or he lives: an immigrant.

In the history of film, aliens are usually seen as those invading the earth in search of natural resources, or in order to abduct humans, to enslave them or to replace human life. H.G. Wells' *The War of the Worlds*,[1] serialised in 1897, was the first work of fiction to describe an alien invasion and the archetype for all science fiction literature that followed. Published in the late 19th century, it is easy to see how it could be read as a harsh critique of European colonialism of that time. The technological superiority of the aliens clearly mimics that of the European powers who were, just as ruthlessly as the Martians in Wells' novel, exploring and exploiting Africa, Asia and the Americas. Wells made countless predictions in respect to the weapons the Martians would use in their attack of Earth. Gas and nuclear weapons were introduced to millions of readers through *The War of The Worlds*, destructive technologies that would only a few years later be used to kill millions of people. It is no coincidence that the *Alien Nation* exhibition brings us back to some of the locations mentioned in Wells' book. Much of the destruction by the aliens took

Orson Welles broadcasting at CBS Radio after the 30 October 1938 radio broadcast of *The War of the Worlds*, November 1938

place in the area in which the ICA is located today, the area around St James's Park, Buckingham Palace, the Houses of Parliament, The Mall and Big Ben were all erased by Martians' lasers. When looking at some of the wonderfully designed covers of various editions of *The War Of The Worlds*, with Big Ben going up in flames, surrounded by flying objects, one cannot help but be reminded of the events of 11 September 2001, when two jet-liners crashed into the Twin Towers of the World Trade Centre in Manhattan and which, in their own way, were also symbols of a conflict based on mistrust, intolerance and radical beliefs.

Many other well-known stories of alien invasions follow, represent or even predict the changing state of current affairs. During the Cold War[2] period, science fiction novels and films, in particular those with the theme of an alien invasion, were frequently used metaphors for the fear of Communist occupation. The film *Invasion of the Body Snatchers* (1956),[3] for example, was seen as a direct critique of McCarthyist[4] paranoia and it comes as no surprise to hear that Daniel Mainwaring, who wrote the screenplay as an adaptation from a novel by Jack Finney, was on McCarthy's infamous blacklist.

The title of this text is taken from the legendary sci-fi TV show *The X-Files*,[5] which perfectly mirrored the excess of conspiracy theories and paranoia surrounding the United States government during the 1990s. It is now a well-known phrase and cultural standard that has inscribed itself into the minds of countless people around the globe. Yet, what that 'truth' might be was never revealed during the ten-year run of the series. Maybe the position of the alien, of being an outcast and stranger, comes with the ability to read and understand the 'truth' (an objective reality of which one is not part) that *The X-Files* promised to reveal, an aptitude which is perhaps shared by aliens and artists alike. It might, therefore, be most appropriate to ask the artists in this exhibition to speak directly and freely about their concerns relating to the issues outlined above, since many of them have referred to science fiction and alien invasion as metaphors for racial discrimination, intolerance and colonialism.

The following statements originate from a series of interviews and conversations that took place over the last 12 months with the artists participating in *Alien Nation*. The questions I posed included

Twin Towers, 11 September 2001

Cover of H.G. Wells' *The War of the Worlds*, 2005

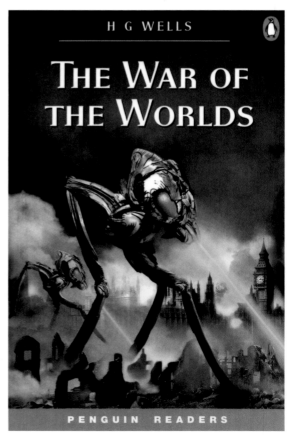

those relating to the general nature of their work and to the specific works selected for the exhibition, as well as those relating to the artists' views and understanding of science fiction. Lastly, I asked the artists whether they ever thought of themselves as aliens and what the term 'alien' means to them within the larger fabric of contemporary society.

Mulder and Skully, *The X-Files*, film still

LAYLAH ALI

I mainly paint and draw, with occasional forays into other areas of working. The drawings for *Alien Nation* are interested in melding and hybridity. They are absurd armless figures that exist in a state of 'post-violence' individualism. Science fiction is always dressed up like it is 'The Future'. It is distant, male and somehow *Star Trek*-like and, as it has been frequently presented by Hollywood and popular paperback fiction and often targeted at a very particular male audience (whose predictable sexual fantasies have become tied up in this sort of fiction), it does not interest me much. So the genre of 'science fiction' is one that I normally do not relate to. One exception would be the iconoclastic work of Octavia Butler, who I think captured the continuum between past, present and future in a way that was more interesting to me. Yes, I suppose I feel like an alien sometimes, as for me it means having big eyes that are constantly searching for clues. That's what I feel like sometimes: a vehicle for my hungry eyeballs. It also means that you are separated from a reliable group dynamic. To be alien is to be – perhaps necessarily – separate and watching.

HAMAD BUTT *

Although this piece of writing has not the intention to cover the production of artworks dealing with AIDS, the propositional aspect of this text will invoke the apprehension of the Triffids of the day.

'All the same', … with a trace of uneasiness, 'is there any particular reason why they should come to just this part in such numbers? I'm sure they do – and I'd like to know just why it is.' (spoken by an apprehensive character in the final chapter, 'Strategic Withdrawal', of John Wyndham's The Day of the Triffids, *Penguin, 1954)*

'They're so different. It seems to me to go against all our ideas of inheritable characteristics…'. (spoken as a reply in the final chapter of John Wyndham's The Day of the Triffids, *Penguin, 1954)*

To remain protected from the danger of the Triffids might mean life on human reservations, a sort of reversal of the usual contaminated concentration camp. We have suspicions of scientific meddling that erupts with blindness to the threats of the origins of the accompanying plague. The Triffids blind their victims, the 'comet' blinds the populace, light in excess blinds the viewer, 'what bursts in the bewilderment of the summit, moreover, as soon as life begins to go astray. The need for an attraction – the necessity, found in the autonomy of human beings, of imposing one's value upon the universe – introduces from the outset a disordered state in all of life'. (George Bataille, Post-scriptum To The Torment (Or The New Mystical Theology), *III Hegel,* Inner Experience, State University Of New York, 1988)

On the cover of the book (of the film, of the television programme) [is] an image of the creature that is not anything as distant as the castrated male genitalia, yet it creeps closer to that dreaded state as it takes the power of mobilization to itself.

And we see the ejaculating approach of blindness, there is the deflation of the 'phallic gaze' with the castration of the 'father-less', which is to say the leader-less masses. Thus they lend themselves to the rule of fear that is generated by the pudenda. With the regard that we pay to the face we see, the blinding of the privileged sense of sight, is the loss that is demanded by the dis-embodied body of the Father's phallus.

Is this the father asking the child for the faithlessness of the sacrifice? The result of the 'impurity' of civilization that is the justification of the myth, 'A story of a world that was wonderfully clever, but so wicked that it had to be destroyed – or destroyed itself by accident? Something like the Flood again'. (John Wyndham, The Day of the Triffids, *Penguin, 1954)*

'… Why pretend it's a myth?'

ELLEN GALLAGHER & EDGAR CLEIJNE

Ellen Gallagher and Edgar Cleijne, *Monster (Murmur)*, 2003–04, 16mm film stills, © Ellen Gallagher / Edgar Cleijne, Courtesy the artists and Hauser & Wirth Zürich London

DAVID HUFFMAN

I consider myself a narrative painter whose practice is drawing and painting. My technique involves laying down a wash that will eventually be populated by a narrative structure executed with drawing, collage and painting. The wash is a nebulous Rorschach simulating an alien environment. All my paintings ebb and flow with formal painting, and social / political science fiction. I create an alphabet of figures that come from diverse media. At times the image will inspire the idea; at other times I seek material that conforms to my idea.

In 1997, I began working with the image of the minstrel, which has morphed over nine years from the depiction of the black-faced minstrel to black characters that populate a narrative composition of interactive exploration. Each body of work is discrete in materiality, but continues the dialogue of minstrel/Traumasmiles (the black figures in action). As the Traumasmiles relate to their environment the paintings require different strategies, i.e. more graphic, different palette, flat v. depth of field. My work is self-referential and very personal. I developed a parallel universe populated by Traumanauts and defensive robots, Luxor Dx and Trauma Eve, who battle in a mythological universe where physical laws are transcended. Not every premise uses all the characters, but they reappear when I feel it necessary for the subject. I mine events, whether historical or contemporary, from various sources, where my metaphoric stories of conflict, enlightenment, fear and resolution combine in muted tones of liquid atmosphere.

It's All Over Now, Baby Blue (2006), a three-panel screen, takes its title from a Bob Dylan song that inspired the cataclysmic epic painted on the screen. I was thinking about the turbulent 1960s, the Vietnam War, the quicksand of contemporary conflicts – indigenous populations overpowered by military might. In short, contemporary socio-political minefields that are played out in my parallel universe of Traumanauts shape the Traumasmiles. The wash was pushed to mimic a charred environment, where the characters are entrenched in a fractured space with several simultaneous military conflicts. My thematic structure is similar to Chinese court paintings and Japanese screen paintings. It's important to note that the wash is the medium for extra-terrestrial space. The laws of physics do not bind the characters: they are free to react in any way I determine. The back of the screen depicts protesters borrowed from the movie *Beneath the Planet of the Apes*, the second of six films about apes evolving from humans. The signs carried by the Traumanauts represent a broad spectrum of oppression, not specific to a time, conflict or cause. Rod Serling was the screenwriter for the production *Planet of the Apes*, and had his own television series, *The Twilight Zone*, where he couched his political/socio agenda. My idea of science fiction is that it is the imagination of science played out in human dramas and I relate to it though the Traumanauts (astronauts) as explorers of their own reality. The Traumanauts exist in a territory that is outside their awareness. I put characters in space suits to be seen as the ultimate visitor, without place (home). The Traumanauts' exploration of self makes them alien everywhere, and to everyone.

HEW LOCKE

I consider myself a bastard child of Kurt Schwitters and Pierre Bonnard. I am like a magpie, picking up inspiration from all sorts of odd sources: from

Baroque churches to Victorian fairgrounds, Portuguese folk festivals to the Macarena Madonna in Seville, palaces in Rajasthan to Hot Wheels cars, and so on.

I work by building in layers – my work is about layers – physical layers relating to layers of meaning; and I work by creating mistakes – I set up problems, which I then need to solve. I change my mind constantly before I start work, and while I am making the work. I allow the material to take me on a journey – I work organically and each piece is a development from a previous piece. I sense that the piece for *Alien Nation* may have a heraldic element to it and I know that I will be using a variety of materials, including wood and toys, and who knows what else. I may do a few sketches to start off – but these are just to get ideas out of my system or to work things out. The main creation goes on in the mind.

My works form a kind of 'invented culture' – something I have been interested in for years. It is about a search – about a doorway into a different reality. This doorway may be found through one tiny seemingly insignificant section of a piece – perhaps a certain shade of green, perhaps a place where two colours come together, or just a shape, or a space. They are extremely elusive these places; they somehow evoke fleeting memories, a feeling almost of déjà vu. My work is about a longing for something you can never reach. Therefore my idea and understanding of science fiction is the creation of another reality that speaks to this reality. I usually relate to sci-fi as entertainment, through films, books or Manga. We are all weird and we are all alien to some extent. Travelling home after an intense day in the studio making portrait heads, the faces of everyone on the Tube look alien and fascinating to me. Some years ago, I was walking down Theobalds Road in London and I looked down a side street to the police station. Above a side entrance there was a lit-up sign that just said 'Aliens' – I never forgot that, it was just weird – just 'what is this'?

MAREPE

My work comes from the observation of materials and situations that repeat daily life and that I dislocate from one context into another. I classify these actions as the synthesis of an idea, using a selective memory as a tool for the work. As an artist I try to give new meaning to the things that are around me, keeping a production line that allows others to have a systematic reading of the works

and to consider a narrative within them. The works made of Christmas ornaments came from my experience of the exhibition *Supletivo Manual, é Natal*, at Galeria Luisa Strina in 2001 in São Paulo. In this show I wanted to reveal the result of a hybrid process in which various cultures come together to form a new one, in which different realities meet. These works also refer to the idea of time, with the relocation of Christmas aesthetics to other periods of the year. Initially, these allegoric sculptures were to be made with glass baubles, but they were replaced by plastic ones that gave me more technical possibilities and a better result for the realisation of the characters.

The Modernist movement in Brazil aimed to bring the Brazilian nation up to date in relation to European ideas of the early 20th century in an anthropophagical way (absorbing the information that was coming from Europe and transforming it for the Brazilian reality). The second and more important movement for us, the 'Tropicalismo' movement, narrowed the relations between Brazil, Europe, America and Africa. I use materials found in the region where I live, and from elsewhere. The materials are not specific to where I live; the same ones are popular in many regions of Brazil and around the world.

My notion of science fiction comes from the movies. I relate to it with curiosity because we are already living much of what was projected as fiction. To feel like an alien is not necessarily an ethnological question but has to do with existential questions. The sensation of being an alien is part of an artist's universe.

HENNA NADEEM

My early experiences as a British Muslim growing up in semi-rural Yorkshire determined the cultural and stylistic motivation of my practice. Nature and landscape formed the backdrop to my childhood, but it was nature viewed through a window rather than experienced directly. Experiencing life indoors and through a window manifested itself in an obsessive collecting of ephemera ... culled from magazines, papers and general stuff bought and found. A marked incongruity about my collection has been the absence of figurative imagery (Islam discourages figurative representation) and my collection reflects that through an emphasis on pattern and landscape.

My current work consists of divergent visual forms, from stand-alone photographs and meticulously handcrafted collages, to semi-functional architectural/sculptural works, digital images and large-scale installations. Linking these forms is an idea of landscape – physical, cultural and psychological, and pattern and decoration. These associations create metaphors for a state of living in modern pluralist Britain. By appropriating imagery from the media, design, popular culture and history; by using multiple references, different scales and values; and by layering culturally and historically exclusive entities, I'm playing with clichés assigned to me as a 'British female Muslim' in an attempt to avoid a fictitious construction of my identity.

A series of small-scale digital montages combines found photographic images of Britain from the 1950s and 1960s with motifs from a range of cultural sources. The work is from a selection of works from *Henna Nadeem: Picture Book of Britain* (a book of montages commissioned and published by Photoworks, Brighton) using super-real colour photographs of the British landscape as my source and inspiration. The montages suggest a familiar but anonymous landscape, shrouded in cut-out forms drawn from a variety of non-western sources. The motifs look as if they are invading the landscape. Two very different visual traditions are woven together to create a new hybrid pictorial space. The work looks at the idyllic British countryside (and cities) at a time before cultural, religious and political changes (through immigration, etc.) become a visible presence in British society. The images focus on the period when my parents and relatives first moved to Britain. The patterns concentrate on motifs that suggest an invasion/observation/union. The montages depict a rural idyll, but beneath the surface there is a suggestion of the landscape being observed or studied in some way. Depending on your point of view, there's a hint of a sense of danger: a lurking presence of some kind, a landscape poised on the brink of an invasion by an alien culture; or, alternatively, the observation may be needed to understand the customs and habits of the nation in order to join, embrace and become a union of mixed cultures and ideals!

My idea of science fiction was formed through watching TV, which played an important part in my childhood. I grew up watching and loving science fiction and horror films. One of my all time favourites is *The Day the Earth Stood Still*. I remember also reading Aldous Huxley's *Brave New World* as part of the school curriculum. Since then I have been drawn

to various sci-fi stories through TV series such as *The Twilight Zone*, *Star Trek* and films like *Invasion of the Body Snatchers*, *Village of the Damned* and *The Fly*, without really seeing myself as a sci-fi fan. I suppose I am attracted to the 'natural sciences' as opposed to the technological or science aspects of sci-fi ... ideas that expand on themes of contact with aliens from other worlds or the biological and mental changes in humans. I see sci-fi as a device that creates an alternate reality, for looking at broader human issues and changes in society and the world as we know it. Sci-fi could be seen as an allegory for my childhood. Enclosed in a small village on the outskirts of Leeds, we observed the locals, but we also made a not always welcome impact on the cosy worlds that we disrupted with our presence.

I was recently thinking about the early 1950s sci-fi movies, which were about the fear and paranoia surrounding the Cold War. That 'threat' has now been replaced with the fear and paranoia of terrorism since the bombing of the World Trade Centre: the Muslim threat. I am also interested in how the presence of something or someone, even when it has long gone, can change the feeling of a place. So, in 2003–04, as part of a residency/commission, I completed a photographic project based around the Tyne and Wear area, north-east England. Here I researched and documented the area where scenes from *Alien 3* were filmed. I wanted to know if the influence of this had affected the landscape.

I actually feel less like an alien than I used to. Living in a pluralistic London allows me to have control and choose my level of alien-ness. I spent most of my formative years feeling like an alien: being part of the only Asian Muslim family in a single faith, single race area, going to a single faith school, listening to single faith prayers, etc. As much as I felt like an alien, I also really felt like a spy or a double agent, except the findings were never reported to anyone ... they were for my own private use. Going to school, absorbing the influences of my peers and then returning home to a strict Muslim household, and vice versa. These separate identities had a strong impact on my life; the different areas had to be balanced but remained quite separate. Never the twain shall meet...

KORI NEWKIRK

How can I possibly describe this thing that I do? I would say I am everyone and no one at the same time: part explorer, scientist, teacher, student, side-show, shaman, employer, employee, carpenter, navigator, writer and reader. It encompasses just about a bit of everything one could ever imagine doing, from the president/CEO down to the person with the absolute worst job. I usually just tell people that I make 'stuff'. This slightly glib answer tends to work well as it leaves it all open ended. But of course it does not always work for everyone, and not every artist needs to make stuff in the same manner that I do. In addition to the 'stuff' I make, I think that as an artist I personally pose questions to the world, questions that while not necessarily needing answers have to in my mind be posed. For *Alien Nation* I will be showing one of the beaded curtains that are a major part of my studio practice. This curtain deviates slightly from the normal form in that it actually depicts '*something*', and by this I mean an '*action*' as compared to the moment being frozen/captured/still. What that something is compared to the other curtains is unknown. I think it is about a moment of transformation/evolution, two areas I have been thinking a lot about for the past few years. They tend to tie into my desire to speak about issues of place and the black body.

I grew up in the 1970s in central New York, and went to a small elementary school on a college campus, which had classrooms with two-way mirrors: children on one side and who knows what or who on the other. Very experimental I guess in its heyday. Anyway, my best friends were obsessed with all sorts of fantasy themed games. I would read stories about dragons and creatures and things, but never really bought all of that as real in any way, and usually shrugged it off as uninteresting to me. So somehow that interest just lay dormant, peaked every few years by this movie or that, a quick glimpse of some Afro funk record cover, pictures of KISS in full makeup, the *Muppet Show* and a favourite aunt who read science fiction books like they were going out of business. My ideas about science fiction evolved from fantasy with the help of yearly showings of the animated versions of *The Lord of the Rings* and *The Lion, the Witch and the Wardrobe*, helped along by the dawning of HBO and reruns of *Logan's Run*, *Dr Who* on PBS and the birth of the *Star Wars* saga.

I feel we are all aliens to some extent. I sit sometimes and watch people and think that we cannot be real, that we must have all come from somewhere else. I certainly hope we did. I am Post-Black Global Negro and, from some of the looks I have gotten over the years, I must be from outer space or something.

YINKA SHONIBARE MBE

As a member of a minority group in the United Kingdom, I have often identified with the alien in popular cinema. Of course it is well known that, at a time when there was a fear of Communism in the USA, Hollywood developed the science fiction genre: films like *Invasion of the Body Snatchers* and *The War of the Worlds* were made. Those films were mostly based on a fear of the dangerous and unknown other. I have also seen films like Steven Spielberg's *Close Encounters of the Third Kind* and *ET* and lived through the ubiquitous fear of UFOs in the 1970s and '80s against a background of nuclear proliferation. I am fascinated by the anthropomorphism of the alien. In cinema and staged photographs of encounters with aliens, the aliens look like us and yet are distinctively different: long necks, big heads, big eyes, etc. The idea of outer space is linked to the human instinct for exploration for economic ends as well as curiosity. Colonialism usually begins as economic exploration before it is eventually followed by imperial power. In a post-colonial period and at a time of contestation for earthly environmental resources, the colonialist impulse is likely to be displaced onto space; perhaps people will take their holidays in space in the future, a subject that features in my work called *Vacation*.

On whether I feel like an alien, of course I do, both as an artist and as a perceived foreigner. Alien-ness is also the source of my creativity, therefore it is a valuable asset: difference rocks. *Dysfunctional Family* (1999) evolved out of an earlier work called *Alien Obsessives*, *Mom*, *Dad and the kids*, a work in which two conventional families of aliens confront each other. In *Dysfunctional Family* I go on to displace the conventional family. Each parent in the partnership is bringing a child from a previous relationship into the new family. The term 'alien' usually refers to foreigners, a term still used on some immigration forms; it also refers to a fear of the unknown or the unknowable.

ERIC WESLEY

The term 'practice' always freaks me out. It makes me nervous like I am a performer or a craftsman, someone who must hone some skill. I think just doing is good enough, or even perfect. For me, it is all about not hesitating and just doing the damn thing. If something pops up, just pull the trigger; instinct will force you to wait until the projectile strikes the heart or the head. As an artist it's all about doing anything and everything you want and not getting caught up in things like medium or money or even emotions. As an artist I feel that what I do is not about what I do, or how or even why I do it. It is about channelling something ... without reason, being the path of least resistance and stepping out of the way. The work I will show in *Alien Nation* deals with the idea of being alienated from peers, superiors, underlings, one's profession, country, race, planet and even one's self. I will set up 'things' to be encountered and worked with by me, the artist, and then presented to you, the viewer. I am tired of making things (being subservient to the object) and am excited about distancing myself from the physical realm of creativity. I want to ditch this antiquated notion of creativity (even if just for some time) and reside in the organisational conceptualism of pure expression.

I relate to science fiction first as a male (as opposed to female) for some reason, then in terms of age. Sci-fi for me is all about ages 9 to about 18. For me it started with dinosaurs, which is so wrong as they do not relate to science or fiction. I would say my relationship with science fiction, which is ongoing, was damaged by my disenchantment with the discipline of the fighter pilot. My outlook on sci-fi now is romantic ... the notion of a great future or some future. Science fiction is, by nature, positive but it is also a bit self-indulging and irresponsible; it's about dreams and dreams are, on the one hand, a liability and, on the other, all there really is. I feel like an alien wherever I go. I think it's positive though; it's sexy and empowering.

MARIO YBARRA JR.

My practice is multi-faceted. I am engaged in several types of art-making. I make images, objects and installations – but most importantly, I make ideas that are the central part of my practice. My work is informed by the relationship with my family, my great-grandparents, my grandparents and their migration to the United States – their language, their moral beliefs and their social values. Also, my work is informed by being American through my parents and my own upbringing in the United States, and the experience and knowledge that that has given me. In terms of its modern incarnation, Mexican–American culture in Los Angeles, where I grew up, has its roots in pre–and post–World War II. Before that time, it strongly identified with the nationalism of Mexico. But, during World War II, during the boom in youth culture and the advent of teenagers, Mexicans formed their own identity. From this point, these kids formed their own language, adopted their own dress code, and formed their own clubs which in turn became the base on which the 1960s and '70s Chicano generation created political groups, low-rider car clubs and street-gang culture. Today, certain aspects of this culture have been exaggerated or exhausted; neo-national organisations are under constant scrutiny for being anti-American. The migrant worker has been reduced to a polarised criminal illegal immigrant and imprisoned gang member or housekeeper. These are the monolithic images that are constantly being shown in media outlets – that is bullshit. There are intellectuals, professionals and avant-garde individuals living in the US who are forwarding new ideological frameworks for not only an existence in the US but also for an existence and resistance globally.

For *Alien Nation*, I will make a mural called *Brown and Proud* (2006), in which I will trace the trajectory of the Mexican historical figure Emiliano Zapata inter-mingled with the George Lucas' *Star Wars* revolutionary figure of Chewbacca – the large brown character that wears a bandolier of bullets like the soldiers of the Mexican Revolution. Science fiction is a place to speculate mythology and the history of human beings in a time/site beyond common knowledge, where species and technology can intermingle. Sometimes, when my psychic ability is working at its best and I receive messages in regard to the interconnectedness with the metaphysical, I almost remember the mission outlines embedded in my brain when the mother-ship beamed me down to Los Angeles.

AND DO NOT FORGET... TRUST NO ONE...

NOTES

1. *The War of the Worlds* (1898), by H.G. Wells, is an early science fiction novel, which describes an invasion of England by aliens from Mars. It is one of the best-known representations of an alien invasion of Earth. The novel was later adapted as a film (1953 and 2005) and as the infamous 1938 radio broadcast by Orson Welles aired as a Halloween special that frightened many listeners into believing that an actual alien invasion was taking place.

2. Emerging after World War II, the Cold War was an extended ideological and economic struggle between capitalism and Communism, centred on the global superpowers of the United States and the Soviet Union. It lasted from about 1947 to the period leading to the collapse of the Soviet Union in 1991.

3. *Invasion of the Body Snatchers* was a science fiction movie made in 1956, directed by Don Siegel, produced by Walter Wanger, and adapted for the screen from a novel by the same title written by Jack Finney.

4. McCarthyism is the term describing a time of intense anti-Communist suspicion in the United States from the late 1940s to the mid to late 1950s, coinciding with increased fears of Communist influence on American institutions and espionage by Soviet agents, as well as the heightened tension from Soviet hegemony over Eastern Europe. The term derives from republican Senator Joseph McCarthy who banded himself as a supreme anti-Communist.

5. *The X-Files* was an American television series created by Chris Carter. The show first aired on FOX in 1993, and ended after a ten-year run on 19 May 2002.

* This extract was written by Hamad Butt in 1990, and published in 'Triffid' in *Hamad Butt: Familiars*, Institute of International Visual Arts (inIVA), London in association with John Hansard Gallery, Southampton, 1996, pp 50–51.

LEFT:
Laylah Ali
Untitled (Types), 2004
Mixed media on paper
27.9 x 19.1 cm
Collection Disaphol Chansiri, Bangkok

RIGHT:
Laylah Ali
Untitled (Types), 2004
Mixed media on paper
27.9 x 19.1 cm
Courtesy Miller Block Gallery, Boston

LEFT:
Laylah Ali
Untitled (Types), 2004
Oil pastel and watercolour pencil on paper
38.1 x 27.9 cm
Collection Daniel and Rena Sternberg, Glencoe, Illinois

RIGHT:
Laylah Ali
Untitled (Types), 2004
Oil pastel and watercolour pencil on paper
27.9 x 19.1 cm
Courtesy Miller Block Gallery, Boston

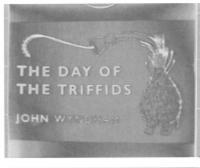  

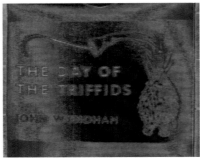  

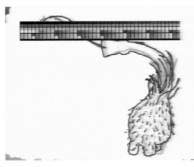  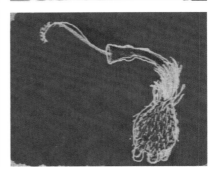

 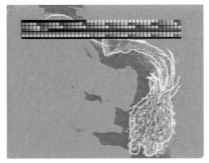 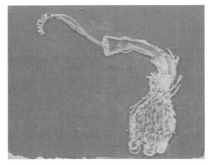

Hamad Butt
The Triffid (part II of the *Transmission* installation), 1990
Film stills from U-matic video transferred to DVD
17 minutes, 8 seconds
Courtesy Ahmad Butt, London

David Huffman
Get Up and Get Down, 2006
Mixed media on paper
127 x 247 cm
Courtesy the artist and Patricia Sweetow Gallery, San Francisco

Hew Locke
Golden Horde, 2006 (details)
Mixed media (plastic, wood, metal and fabric)
Dimensions variable
Courtesy the artist and Hales Gallery, London

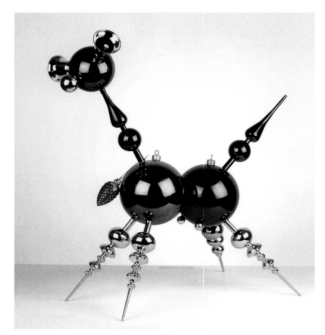

TOP LEFT:
Marepe
Untitled, 2002
Christmas ornaments
53 x 20 x 32 cm
Private Collection, London

TOP RIGHT:
Marepe
Untitled, 2002
Christmas ornaments
65 x 60 x 44 cm
Collection Steven D. Corkin, Boston

BOTTOM LEFT:
Marepe
Untitled, 2002
Christmas ornaments
29 x 50 x 30 cm
Courtesy Galeria Luisa Strina, São Paulo

BOTTOM RIGHT:
Marepe
Untitled, 2002
Christmas ornaments
70 x 50 x 26 cm
Courtesy Galeria Fortes Vilaça, São Paulo

Henna Nadeem
Plan, 2006
Digital montage
Image size 31.5 x 36 cm
Commissioned by Photoworks
Courtesy the artist and Photoworks

Kori Newkirk
Drawing for *Merk*, 2006
Computer-generated drawing
Courtesy the artist and The Project, New York

Eric Wesley
Plan for *Untitled*, 2006
Computer-generated drawing
Courtesy the artist

Mario Ybarra Jr.
Sketch for *Brown and Proud*, 2006
Graphite on paper
Courtesy the artist

Ellen Gallagher and Edgar Cleijne
Monster (Murmur), 2003–04
16mm film stills
© Ellen Gallagher / Edgar Cleijne, Courtesy the artists
and Hauser & Wirth Zürich London

MURMUR: MEDITATIONS, FICTIONS AND FORENSICS FOR INVISIBLE AMERICANS BY GREG TATE

Sexuality formed the nexus in which black, female, sexuality and chattel were inextricably bound and acted to intensify the constraints of slave status by subjecting the body to another order of violations and whims. The discourse of seduction enabled those disgusted and outraged by the sexual arrangements of slavery, like Mary Boykin Chestnut, to target slave women as the agents of their husband's downfall.

'Under slavery we live surrounded by prostitutes, yet an abandoned woman is sent out of any decent house. Who thinks any worse of a Negro or mulatto woman for being a thing we can't name?'

The sexuality of the enslaved female, incredulously, served as evidence of her collusion with the master class and as evidence of her power, the power both to render her master weak and be the mistress of her own subjection.
(Saidiya V. Hartman, Scenes of Subjection, Terror, Slavery, and Self-Making in Nineteenth-Century America)

So important a silence as their lives dwindled, rusted, corrupted away.
As the port where the smoke rises for the poor french sailor and his indian whore.
There are bones, which still clog those blue soft seas
and give a human history to nature. Can you understand
that nothing is free! Not even the floating strangeness of the poet's head
the crafted visions of the intellect, named, controlled, beat and erected to work, and
struggle under the heavy fingers of art. What valley, what mountain, what eagle or
afternoon, is not fixed or changed under our feet or eyes?
(Le Roi Jones/Amiri Baraka, 'Green Lantern's Solo')

Double consciousness is a bitch. Black being means never having to invoke the alien imaginary. Tag, you're IT. The thing that can't even be named, live and in living binary colours. The thing, seen through a glass darkly, finds its opposite held in thrall too. Visions of Toni Morrison echoing in its head: 'If you're going to hold someone down you're going to have to hold on by the other end of the chain. You are confined by your own repression.' The dark side of the moon, no different from the light, scorched and pitted rock, torched by the flaming offal of long dead stars. Thanks to our grand literary tradition of Gothic anxiety only to the dark side has descended the poetic depth charge, the metaphoric and prophetic weight of storm clouds gathering. But history also provides ample proof that the light will not be denied its devilish due. For every Darth Vader a Children of the Corn, for every Kong a Fay Wray, for every Lulu a Blonde Venus, for every Kennedy a Marilyn Monroe. Before 19th-century slave revolt leader Nat Turner was hung, skinned and his castrated body parts dispersed to his attendant lynch mob for pickled souvenirs – well before all that – he told his counsel/confessor/interlocutor, Thomas Gray, that his famous rampage was preceded by dreams of dewy blood drops sprinkled over acres of golden cornstalks and black spirits battling white spirits high in the antebellum skies. Yet the most bizarre moment in the text – Turner's actual confessions (not to be confused with the less phantasmagorical Styron novel) – occurs after Turner offers up his parents' belief that his mystic gifts derived from 'certain marks on my head and breast'. Even more odd, though, is attorney Gray's bracketed diagnoses of Turner's ascribed facial markings: '[a pracel of excrescences which I believe are not at all uncommon, particularly among negroes, as I have seen several with the same. In this case he has either cut them off, or they have nearly disappeared]'. You want to reach back, haul back, hit this fool with 'Your mama's an excrescence'. Like, what cauliflower-headed *Star Trek: The Next Generation* Klingon Negro was this fool hallucinating about in 1831? A radical species 'disappeared' after Turner's body got dissected and dumped in with the planter's family jewels? Indeed, at this point in the narrative, one begins to ask who's having the psychotic break here, the teller or the whaler, the rebel or his revelator? You are reminded of Ellison's *Invisible Man* when the narrator Others his Cyclopean commie interrogator as a monster, but is later given to wonder which eye is really the blind one when it comes to where Caucasoids and close encounters of the Negro kind are concerned. You are also reminded of those passages in *The Wretched of the Earth* where Fanon condemns African mysticism as a 'phantasmal plane' constructed to deny the reality of colonial oppression. What would Fanon have made of woolly-headed Turner and his amanuensis Gray? A duet, who in concert beg the question of just who is the scientist and who is the fiction? Turner reveals this about his childhood: 'All my time not devoted to my master's service, was spent either in prayer, or in making experiments in casting different things in moulds made of earth, in attempting to make paper, gunpowder, and many other experiments, that although I could not perfect, yet convinced me of its practicability if I had the means.' Turner, Gray tells us, proved remarkably well informed when questioned on these matters.

Octavia Butler and Samuel Delany, the world's premier sci-fi writers of African descent, both enjoy depicting the Protean and Ovidean instability of racial identities. Both also are smitten by the beguiling powers of racial exoticism and narcissism. The sci-fi imaginary, so often turning on encounters between humans and superior aliens, is given a racialised turn in Delany's and Butler's work. In their fictions, the aliens found among us are not only smarter but also sexier, and more visionary. This sensual conception of higher alien intelligence brings to mind James Baldwin being asked if he thought Negroes were superior to white people and Baldwin replied, 'No', but he believed 'we people who are darker than blue' (per Curtis Mayfield's coinage) had 'a greater capacity for experience'. This in turn recalls the rap where Gil Scott Heron, the Hegel of proto-hiphop, describes himself as a 'bluesologist': one who traffics in the 'science of how things feel'. Apropos here since Delany and Butler share an obsession with representing their human / alien (or mutation) encounters as quite tactile: as a thing that gets under the skin, not to anally probe terrestrial bodies (for homoerotic panic reflexes no doubt), but to wantonly transform human desires into alien desires, to provoke repulsion/attraction for dispossessive alien touches. Delany and Butler, masterfully rewriting the whole sadomasochistic history of totem and taboo peculiar to American slavery and its discontents, have repeatedly given us superior alien Others who've come not to conquer our planet but overwhelm our sexual agency and mating urges – to haunt, complicate, obliterate the distance between difference and desire, self and other, species and mutation. Sci-fi's familiar trope, 'looks that can kill', is gaily transformed by Delany and Butler into traumas that can objectify you right out of your skin. Autogenocide becomes the new social control mechanism. Slaves are made to rationalise and normalise the invasive species-erasing powers of master Others. But double consciousness, that Afro-Manichean neurosis Cecil Taylor once indicted in the phrase 'dark to themselves', remains intact, a brain-zapping bitch, our species surviving self-memory refusing to give up the ghost to any old alien transmogrification of the flesh. (A brain-zapping bitch, robotically firing blanks in mental terrain more austere than a proper Muslim graveyard, maggot brains on parade, where evolution goes to see a side-show, moist, moulting, light-projected… The dream-life of antennae, of amniocentesis, of amoebas with dirty faces … as detailed as Hartman demands if we are to recognise 'the fungibility of the captive body'.)

'EVERY WAR, CRISIS, WITCH-HUNT, RACE RIOT AND PURGE, IS A REMINDER AND WARNING. WE ARE THE MARTIANS. IF WE CANNOT CONTROL THE INHERITANCE WITHIN US, THIS WILL BE THE SECOND DEAD PLANET.'

RUDOLPH CARTIER, DIR. *QUATERMASS AND THE PIT*
(BBC, LONDON, 1958–59)

'The Monstrousness That Reigns Here': Quatermass and 'The Anglicisation of Outer Space' by David Alan Mellor

Introduction: The Figure of the Scientist

Like Mary Shelley's *Frankenstein*, Nigel Kneale's *Quatermass* series, broadcast by BBC TV between 1953 and 1959 as *The Quatermass Experiment*, 1953 (hereafter *QE*); *Quatermass II*, 1955 (*QII*), and *Quatermass and the Pit*, 1958–59 (*QP*), took a scientist's name as its title. The fictional Professor Bernard Quatermass incarnated a specifically British imperial ascetic ideal of public service – like Conrad's policeman in *The Secret Agent*, as well as being a forensic figure, like Sherlock Holmes, fully embracing positivist science. But, as an agent of the dominant rationality, Quatermass is perpetually confronted with its underside, its unspeakable verso, contained in empirical evidence which will threaten to make him insane[1] by raising metaphysical perspectives of some alien evil – what Martin Heidegger, characterising the affective structure generated by contemporary technology, called in 1955, 'the monstrousness that reigns here'.[2]

The tele-fictional figure of Quatermass has the charisma of a British Wernher Von Braun, a human with a preternatural grasp of science and technology.[3] By controlling – ultimately unsuccessfully – the secrets of atomic power for his first rocket, the *BR7*, Quatermass is given an altogether exceptional status – he is a seer, an ascetic, a dark and fugitive man, like the figure in the 1946 *Picture Post* photograph of the magician-like pioneer of Britain's initial atomic energy programme, Professor John Cockcroft.[4] Cockroft, readers were told, was an uncanny technological supremo who worked on ominous ancient ground, foreshadowing Quatermass' encounter with the lethal deep past a decade later in *QP*. The caption for the introductory photo-portrait of a vampiric Cockroft read: 'The Man in Charge goes Strolling on the site of Britain's First Atomic Pile/His name is Professor John Cockroft. His walk takes him out of Harwell onto Berkshire ridges studded with the relics of more than one dead civilisation…'.

The Imaginary Spaces and Visual Styles of Quatermass: Brutalism and Biomorphic Horror

The dramatic novelties of the emergent technological landscapes of the 1950s – the Berkshire nuclear plants, the Thames estuary oil refineries, the new build Heathrow Airport complex – found currency in representations of a modernising Britain entering what was touted as a 'New Elizabethan Age', with the coronation of Queen Elizabeth II just three months before production began on *QE*. But the gross facticity of concrete constructions and arrays of piped metallic assemblages and antennae – the universe of strange new Britishness, which was seen in the *Quatermass* series – countered the popular romance of monarchic renewal. There were, of course, exceptions, such as the Commonwealth pageant of technology and exploration epitomised by the radio-photographs of the goggled and protective suited figures of the New Zealander, Edmund Hillary, and the Nepalese, Tenzing Norkay (or Tensing Bhutia), just below the summit of Mt Everest in time for newspaper reproduction on the morning of the coronation. Masked and with breathing apparatus, Hillary resembled the drawings of projected spacemen, which had been appearing in magazines for at least the past year.

Set of crashed spaceship and ruined house
The Quatermass Experiment, 1953, set photograph

Two visual styles dominate the décor and appearance of the *Quatermass* series. The first was a version of what sculptors and architects were dubbing 'The New Brutalism': a harsh factualism of materials and contemporary technical objects seen in the buildings of the Smithsons and the sculpture of Eduardo Paolozzi; the second was another modernist style, exemplified in the paintings of Graham Sutherland and Kneale's brother, Bryan, a style descended from Surrealism: Biomorphism. Both pictorial codes – Brutalism and Biomorphism – were the successors to the nostalgic Neo-Romantic figurative style of the 1940s in British art.[5] As *QII* opened, Kneale questioned the power of this idyllic landscape Neo-Romantic iconography by placing a vast elm in leaf in the corner of a field in juxtaposition to radar scanners and dishes, to Army Land Rovers and trucks, near where lethal asteroids will fall, infecting a ploughman. It did not simply take extra-terrestrial invaders (from one of the moons of Saturn) to transform the Neo-Romantic rural and urban landscape of Britain into *unheimlich* territory; this had been successfully achieved, in the serial, by governmental imposition of temporary Modernist pre-cast concrete architecture – prefabs – transforming the workers' housing at the fictive Winnerden Flats into 'A strange place … a very strange place'.

Brutalism was born out of a renewal of the built civic fabric so badly damaged by the devastations of war from Blitz and V2 rocket attacks. The construction of new office blocks in Knightsbridge, in 1957, were the locus point for Kneale's inspiration for *QP*: 'Suppose a building contractor was excavating a site for a big office block and going really deep… and suddenly came across what looked like a space ship. … I set it in Knightsbridge because it was being rebuilt at great speed, and again it had great holes and people digging down, a hundred feet'.[6] The set designs to realise the BBC's *QP* were undertaken by Clifford Hatts, and the Brutalist naturalism of his 1958 sets – construction sites; the half-demolished terraced houses of Hobbs Lane; London clay soil on display and the inclusion of TV cameras in shot – has particular resonance in terms of British avant-garde Brutalism of the 1950s. As the then Head of BBC TV Design, Richard Levin's 1961 commentary on *QP* presented Hatts' raw realism as the guarantee of the credibility of the science fiction narrative: 'a setting of such complete and unremarkable authenticity as to make the fantasy just possibly believable'.[7]

Similarly, in Richard Hamilton's contemporary paintings, such as *Hommage à Chrysler Corp.* (1957), a conjunction was effected between the bug-eyed monster of science fiction – the 'BEM' – and the sanctioning apparatus of built and manufactured construction. The blistered forms of technical intelligence found in Clifford Hatts' design for the Martian rocket in *QP* may owe something to the multiple facets and techno-blisters of the Zeiss Projector which lay at the heart of the new (1957) London Planetarium: 'Although the thirty third to leave a German factory it is the first to be erected in the British Common-wealth. The instrument … looks like some brooding two-headed monster from outer space…'.[8] The brochure of the new Planetarium made plain how far elements of ex-Nazi technological expertise, fleeing from baleful Soviet seizure, and taking on new identities as West Germans, were present in the Zeiss optical machinery in Baker Street: '…more and more workers made their way from the Russian zone to rejoin their colleagues in Western Germany. Today the Zeiss factories are producing an unbelievably large range of apparatus of which the mighty Planetarium Instrument is but one example'.[9] Everywhere – in this public relations text, for example, or in the tenantless terraces of Hobbs Lane – there were signs of human dispersal and dispossession, signs of expulsion in the face of brutal and ruthless modernities, giving rise to a sense of unroofed unhomeliness, generating the uncanny in relation to advanced technologies.

The crashed spaceship in the pit set, *Quatermass and the Pit*, 1958–59, set photograph

The dome and the 'universal projector' of the London Planetarium, which had been first mooted in 1950, were vital additions to the visual forms and signs of 'space consciousness', which began, in the early 1950s, to compose a vocabulary of images which would structure the imagination of space travel and the othernesses that would be encountered in this extension of the colonial urge. In part this was a development of the imagery of modernisation which pervaded the 1950s, and in the brochure of the London Planetarium, published in 1957, the construction of the dome is shown in photographs, which not only echo the construction boom in office blocks in central London in the late 1950s, but also the 'excavations' and rudimentary shelter of Group 6 in the Whitechapel Gallery exhibition, *This is Tomorrow* and the excavation for the set of *QP*.[10] It was claimed, in the context of the re-making of London in the 1950s, that the new Planetarium, projecting its simulations of outer space onto the interior hemisphere of the dome was 'London's most modern building which houses the entertainment of the future'.[11]

So the future collided with the remnants, debris and strata of the past. There were strong associations between Hatts' weird construction site design for *QP* and the back garden lean-to and discarded archaeologically-resonant fragments created by Nigel Henderson and Paolozzi for *This is Tomorrow*. Just as Henderson's own Bethnal Green terraced house and back garden were the model for his 'Patio and Pavilion', the set of *QP* evoked the diminishing working class housing stock of inner London in the rhetoric of unhomely Brutalism: 'The camera pans to take in all that remains of a little working class street. Most of it has been demolished … only five of the small terrace-houses are left and their demolition is clearly imminent. That farthest from the corner is a roofless ruin … and the street itself is stacked with cement bags, grab-chains, stacks of reinforcing metal, scaffolding, sand'.[12]

Martians suspended in the crashed spaceship's front cabin, *Quatermass and the Pit*, 1958–59, set photograph

Biomorphic Visual Metaphor

Kneale's younger brother, Bryan, while not being included in the choice of British sculptors for the Venice Biennale of 1952, which announced the 'Geometry of Fear' style, nevertheless worked in the idiom which Chadwick, Meadows and others made internationally celebrated – with references to crustacea and organic mutations – in a new British style of spiky Biomorphism. This was six years before Jack Kine and Bernard Wilkie, the BBC TV special effects men who worked on the *Quatermass* series, were directed to model the Martians who would haunt *QP* from a Biomorphic painting of a lobster, which Bryan Kneale then had on exhibition at the Redfern Gallery in London. Bryan Kneale took up sculpture in 1959, with *Armour* (1960) being his first significant work: like a less naturalistic version of Kine's and Wilkie's Martian, it was another totemic 'hybrid of anthropomorphic and vegetal forms, which Kneale claimed reflected certain experiences from his sub-conscious'.[13] The one conspicuous precedent for the 'Geometry of Fear' sculpture, for Kine's and Wilkie's tripod-legged Martian, and for Kneale's sculpture *Armour* was Jacob Epstein's *Rock Drill* of 1913–14. This sculpture was an inescapable template for British post-World War II sculptors who reconciled romantic organic nightmares with metallic rationalisation. Epstein himself had recognised the genetic issue of nesting alien life within a technological shell and the uncanniness that resulted: it was '…a machine-like robot, visored, menacing and carrying within itself its progeny, protectively ensconced. Here is the armed and sinister figure of today and tomorrow. No humanity, only the terrible Frankenstein's monster we have made ourselves into'.[14]

It was David Sylvester, in 1956, who first pointed out the links between the *Quatermass* series and contemporary Biomorphic sculpture, as well as the essential organic abjection which characterised the appearance of Caroon, the returning English spaceman in *QE*:

'...it is a creature in a state of metamorphosis from human being into plant. Moreover, its form of aggression is altogether inhuman ... whatever living organism he touches "has the life drained out of it" ... he strikes a cactus and his arm is transmuted into a cactoid growth'.[15] Sylvester's analysis of the first two *Quatermass* serials (and their film adaptations) located them fully in the iconography and space of contemporary art. He began by comparing Caroon's hybrid cactus arm to a sculpture by Germaine Richier 'of a human figure one of whose arms is the branch of a tree. The arm itself at this stage, a pulpy mass with spikes sticking out of it, calls to mind a particular *Thorn Head* by Graham Sutherland, which has similar spikes and a pulpy mass at the centre. At the next stage in its transformation, when all we see of it is a glimpse of its face through the shrubbery and a sight of the trail of slime it leaves behind it, we are likely to be reminded of certain paintings by Francis Bacon done about six or seven years ago in which the human face and figure are translated into a kind of clotted grey protoplasm'.[16]

This terminal horror, this state of abjection – rooted in those same amorphous, indeterminate, contaminative materials which Sylvester read off from Bacon's paintings – constitutes one of the affects of dread and anxiety in the *Quatermass* series. A poisonous black slime, deadly to the unprotected human body, is the perverse nutrient for the colonising aliens in *QII*. Prior to this, the aliens are marked as excremental since their small rock asteroid vehicles 'Stink, like dirty stables'. The fresh techno-modernity of the Shell oil refinery, in its role as the super-factory for synthetic food, contains the site for the manufacture of this corrosive slime, a 'protected colony' for nurturing the unspeakable aliens, like the maternal metal shell of Epstein's *Rock Drill*. The domes where the aliens are nourished recall the dome of the Windscale facility in Cumbria from which weapons grade plutonium had been generated, providing the core for 'Hurricane' Britain's first atomic bomb, tested at the Australian Monte Bello Isles in June 1952.[17] This is a site charged with horror and Kneale's script outlines the aliens in the language of a sublime abjection: 'Shapes that have no shape ... but which, to judge by the size of the lamps in the dome ... are colossal. Something slithers like a mudfish, puffs to a dripping grey protuberance as high as a man – shoots upwards ... a bobbing bladder distends itself into a vast glistening cloud. ...A monstrous, swaying column of glistening living matter rises past the inspection window... plunges, sending the black ooze spattering against the glass'.[18]

Sir Jacob Epstein, *Torso in Metal from 'The Rock Drill'*, 1913–14, bronze   Bryan Kneale, *Crayfish*, 1955, oil on canvas

FOURPENCE-
HALFPENNY

EVERY FRIDAY

EAGLE

4 JULY 1952 Vol. 3 No. 13

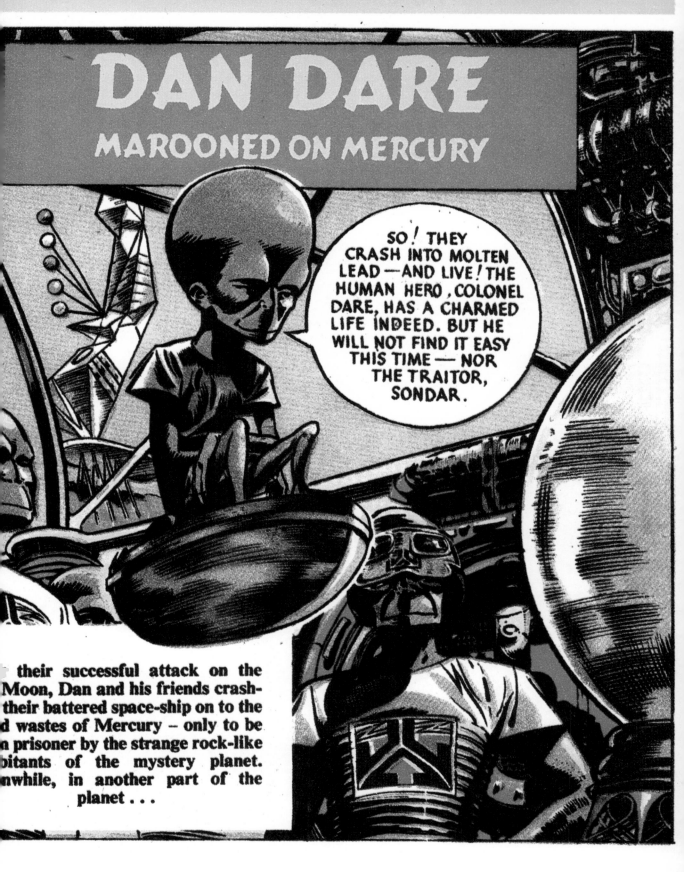

The End of One Empire: Another One in Space?

When Quatermass begins to realise the enormity of the horror that has consumed two of the spacemen on board his *BR7* rocket in *QE*, he turns to camera in a close shot – a pale, sombre, gaunt figure. Then he soliloquises on the forfeited colonial life, which he might have led had he not become a physicist and rocketeer: 'Thirty years ago I was going to devote myself to land surveying in the tropics'. Now the measuring of newer, colonial boundaries eludes him when faced with the incommensurable distances of outer space, those unimaginable, sublime dimensions where monstrousness reigns and seizes the western human. Professor Bernard Quatermass, as impersonated in 1953 by the first actor to take the role, Reginald Tate, was a recognisable figure drawn from the landscape of 20th-century British types: the neurotic, spare, innovative and impatient imperial adventurer, a saviour figure at odds with the managed phase of the Commonwealth, a T.E. Lawrence or an Orde Wingate. Tate was a veteran RFC aviator from the Great War, one of the nervous techno-gladiators flying free of the earth, ascensional, as Kneale recognised: 'He had to be almost quasi-religious…'.[19] The limits of white, western exploration and colonisation were reached, in *QE*, when contact was made with another predatory, colonising culture, whose tendrils ultimately reach into the symbolic centre of Commonwealth and imperial British rule, Westminster Abbey, where Queen Elizabeth II had been crowned only two months before.

The technological mythologies, which were seen to distinguish the so-called 'New Elizabethan Age', clothed the explorations and conquests of a post-war British state in the romanticised outward forms of the heroic age of 16th-century imperialism, of '…the great knight-errants of the sea'.[20] The soaring flight of the nuclear-powered *BR7*, which opens *QE*, carries the patriotic *afflatus* (soon to be dashed) into the skies like the doomed jet passenger aircraft, the Comet. These jet and rocket pilots, like Caroon, were analogous with the merchant-

Professor Quatermass and his team supporting the surviving spaceman, *The Quatermass Experiment*, 1953, set photograph

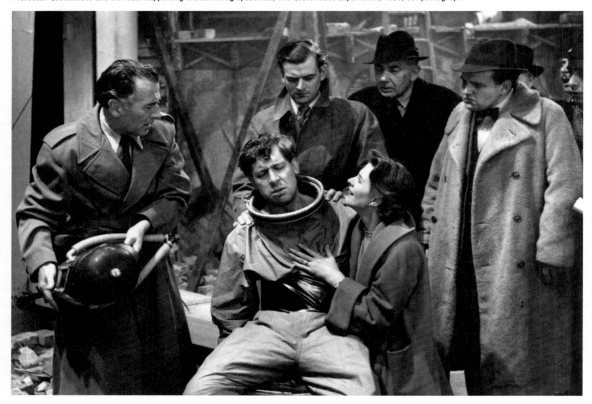

adventurers borne on the Thames whom Conrad described: '…what greatness had not floated on the ebb of the river into the mystery of an unknown earth! … the dream of men, the seed of commonwealth, the germs of empires'.[21] Politically and culturally, this aspirational neo-colonial questing rhetoric of a 'new frontier' – which particularly flourished in the reformist ambitions of JFK's presidency, from 1961 onwards – had, in fact, been predated by an explosion of fantasmic space-colonial language, c.1951–52. While in the USA Wernher von Braun presented his arguments for building rockets to explore outer space primarily in terms of national security, in Britain Arthur C. Clarke used well-worn motifs of colonial exploration, developments of Wells' utopian idealism over space travel in *The Shape of Things to Come*, of almost 20 years before: 'But men have never failed to respond to any challenge Nature can provide. The next few centuries will see the conquest of the planets… And then new frontiers will beckon, and the endless march will begin again'.[22] Thus the *Quatermass* series 'take-off' from that post-war Atlanticist public fascination with space travel and rocketry, which stems the moment in 1951–52 when a cluster of publications map speculative future histories. Arthur C. Clarke's *Interplanetary Travel* (1951) becomes America's 'Book of the Month' in March 1952, when a spate of magazine articles publicise the colonisation of outer space in the language (in Britain at least) of imperial colonisation and travel. In Britain, *Picture Post* carries Arthur C. Clarke's articles in the spring and summer of that year,[23] while between 1952 and 1954 the American magazine, *Colliers*, has been credited with 'setting the agenda NASA follows to this day',[24] beginning in its 22 March 1952 issue, 'Man Will Conquer Space Soon'.

The Cold War emergency of the Korean War probably found its outer-space allegory in the narrative of the British hero, Colonel Dan Dare, in the new boys' magazine, *Eagle*. The Communist invasion of South Korea in 1950 moved NATO and the UN into 'total mobilisation', one that accelerated the process of re-armament to which the Atlee government had committed in 1949. But in the course of 1951, British and American troops, facing overwhelming numbers of Chinese Communists, were forced to retreat down the Korean peninsula, to the point where the Allied Commander, General MacArthur, advised the using of atomic weapons. The political emergency was reflected in the British Prime Minister Clement Atlee's race to Washington to counter such an escalation. It is at this moment that the *Eagle* calls the British 'pilot of the future', Dan Dare, 'back to London, back to lead an expedition to discover the terrible secret of the RED MOON – the new number one mystery of the universe, back to fight a peril even more deadly than the Treens!'.[25] Dare commands space rockets for the Space Fleet, a multinational, United Nations-type force of westerners – an American, a Lancashire batman, a Frenchman – representatives of those colonial powers who, in the early and mid-1950s, were beleaguered by the gathering forces of insurgency in Kenya, Korea and Indo-China.

So the empire was recoiled from; but always – and most obviously with the British/French /Israeli invasion of Egypt in 1956, the Suez débâcle – the temptation to re-impose imperial fiat in hostile space insinuated itself. 'Whoever plants those bases can police the earth', Colonel Breen exults, referring to Quatermass' planned Moon and Mars colonies, at the War Office Conference at the beginning of *QP*. He utters these words under a large official portrait photograph of HM The Queen, whose picture is in line with photographs of Mars and the Moon. A new imperial adventure to 'police the Earth' by rocket ship and nuclear warheads appeared to be underway in fiction and fact: in August 1958 the American outline military strategy of using the Moon's surface as a new fortress, a secure 'high ground' – itself a development of von Braun's earth-orbit military panopticism for which he propagandised a few years earlier[26] – was disclosed to English readers of *The New Statesman*. The science writer, Ritchie Calder, wrote in his regular space science column that 'US generals are now talking of the Moon as a new Gibraltar'.[27]

The boardroom with photographs of HM The Queen, Mars and the Moon, *Quatermass and the Pit*, 1958–59, set photograph

In these transformations of power and its vantage points of Earth and space, it was post-war venture finance capitalism that was remorselessly reshaping London by commercial office building in the late 1950s. Re-figured, in *QP*, this would be the unwitting instrument for another colonial reflux: a genocidal Martian project to colonise a metropolis-to-be of primaeval swamps from millions of years before: this was the ancient Thames Valley which had been the location of Marlow's musing in Joseph Conrad's *Heart of Darkness*. This novel used the metaphoric reciprocities of colonial spaces and time, which superimposed the Thames of the beginning of the 20th century onto the 1st century AD and the Congo: 'And this also', said Marlow suddenly 'has been one of the dark places of the earth'.[28]

The iconography of the *Quatermass* series was replete in varieties of this metaphoric darkness – a 'darkness' that unsteadily mirrored tropes of race and primitivism and their representations. In *QII*, those marked as alien creatures are branded by a 'big, black bubble' which, in the Hammer film version, is a delicate and decorative patterned curvilinear thing, close to a Maori decoration, but superimposed upon a European physiognomy. This 'black bubble' leaves the stain of another race, of the expressive forms and signs of the 'aboriginals', those who still, vestigially, populated the Commonwealth rocket firing zones of Emu and Woomera. This annexation of tribal signs is utilised again in *QP* when the palaeontologist, Dr Matthew Ronay, invites Quatermass to examine a face from reproductions of what are African Kalahari Bush people's paintings of hunts, reproductions which he has as a mural running across his laboratory wall. His implicit comparison is with the Biomorphic, Epstein-esque 'Martian', now chemically embalmed and standing upright, in juxtaposition with them. Ronay says: 'How do you like our décor?… They are copies of palaeolithic cave painting … about 30,000 years old. Look at that one – a cave man in a ritual mask… (*knowingly*). You know, I think they (the Martians) are friends we haven't seen for a long time'. In these examples, instances of extra-European visualities become stand-ins for the uncanny – something known of old but now taking on a radically alien appearance.

But it is the metaphor of darkness and blackness that circulates most effectively through the series. In *QII*, the extra-terrestrial invaders exist in 'a freak orbit on the dark side of the earth'. Where Quatermass' real-world model and later Cold War warrior, Sir Bernard Lovell, had sought white radar traces of falling meteors on his CRT screens, Quatermass, in the film version of *QII*, finds black traces, falling across his screens – computable but anonymous, insidious traces. Perhaps – in this *lapsus* of the image, this blackness – the 1950s series registers a post-empire Windrush allegory of invasion across familiar urban and rural landscapes and of the decanting of invaders into containing sanctuaries for incubation? The amorphous and toxic alien creatures in *QII* exist in 'protected colonies'. Related to this are Kneale's imaginative refigurings of immigration by aliens: the journalist Conrad, losing his fight to be free from their invasive influence, announces to his news desk, 'We're coming, we're coming'. Again, in *QII*, Professor Quatermass notices the fall of many asteroids, from the vantage of an English pub: 'They're coming in their thousands, this is it'. The horror of contamination by these dark traces is again figured in *QII* during a clandestine visit to the synthetic food plant at Winnerden Flats, where a public relations officer gains close contact with the product and is turned black from head to foot, leaving a black trace, a smear from his hands passing over the bright white surfaces of the chemical installation. The crucial aspect of this transformation of genteel members of ruling English élites into black-faced figures was the texture of their new corporeality: it is an abject blackness of slime or oil or tar, another marker of the verso of technology. This is a sinister darkness, without question, like the amorphous dark shapes seen by Quatermass himself in the TV version, or the towering animate black creatures who are released at the climax of the film version of *QII*.

Professor Quatermass and Dr Matthew Ronay in the lab, *Quatermass and the Pit*, 1958–59, set photograph

The Chthonic and Territories of Dispossession

In 1912, British imperial primacy in the world was bolstered by apparent discovery, at Piltdown in Sussex, of the earliest hominid skulls. Piltdown – and its dubious resonances – is refound in the opening sequence of *QP*, with an African workman – Jack, played by the actor Lionel Ngakane – as part of the gang of navvies digging out the excavation for the office block in Knightsbridge. Kneale had worked hard to get an African actor included in the serial, appalled at the reigning prejudice against casting blacks.[29] Ngakane is presented by Kneale in a Hamlet-like moment of memento mori reflection – wondering if the skull belonged to someone who 'might 'a been murdered'.[30] To the metaphors of darkness was added a structure of spectralisation which follows on from that discourse of territorial dispossession which also circulates in the *Quatermass* series, a dispossession which can be, and, in *QP* is, located in the deep pre-historic past. Here was an intersection with a massive Darwinian narrative. A primal, aboriginal Britain of the early hominid species had been the site of historical struggle and even forgery – in 1953, Piltdown Man was comprehensively discredited as a hoax at the Department of Geology at the British Museum and evidence exhibited at the Natural History Museum (the future fictional location of Dr Ronay's Nicklin Institute of Research in Natural History, where he will identify the genetically altered hominids of *QP*). It was an imperial object of speculation and fascination – H.G. Wells had imagined the displacement and extermination of Neanderthal Man, in the English landscape, just as, in *The War of the Worlds*, he forecast the possibility of advanced industrial *homo sapiens* being exterminated by displaced aliens, in an allegory of contemporary colonial expansion.

The terror and murderousness, which Jack feared as the context for the Knightsbridge skull in *QP* in 1958, was at the centre of an actual epochal excavation, in the Olduvai Gorge in Kenya. The discovery of extremely archaic weaponry at Olduvai by Louis Leakey had been regularly featured in British magazines, such as *The Illustrated London News* through the 1940s and 1950s, but it was his discoveries of 1957–58 which were decisive in suggesting fabulously early dates for hominid life stretching back half a million years, refining his 1946 uncoverings of Acheulean hand-axe makers who hunted giant baboons. In July 1958 Leakey could announce: 'We have now found and studied two living sites of Chellean Man … Hitherto we had thought of man starting to use ivory for tool making only in the Upper Palaeolithic a mere 30,000 years ago. Now we find he started to do so nearly half a million years ago'.[31] Africa was now the *loci* of studies of prehistoric life, from the monstrous Coelacanth caught off Madagascar on 20 December 1954, which had been believed to be extinct 50,000,000 years ago, to the archaic Chellean hominid of Oldevai, who flourished half a million years before: these were chthonic, mythic discoveries and something of their significance is evident in the special aura of the ominous finding of the skulls at the outset of *QP*.

In 1952 a State of Emergency was declared in Kenya and photographs of aerial surveillance to try to police the open farmed landscape from Mau Mau insurgents was featured in the British press, particularly after the slaughter of the Ruck settler family in December 1952. Policing terror had an optic – the 'high ground', high level view of the Colonial Air Patrols which showed in *The Illustrated London News*: 'A trim but isolated European homestead in Kenya – from the air – with left, native workers huts which Mau Mau turned into a source of uneasy doubt'.[32] This was the Kenyan context for the epoch-making palaeontology discoveries of the pre-history of early man by 'a son of Kenya',[33] Louis Leakey. The aspect of colonial horror may have been part of the reception of Leakey's discoveries of early hominids and possibly it colours the palaeontology in *QP*. Born and raised in what would become insurgent Kikuyu territory, Leakey was also the former head of Special Branch in the Nairobi CID and was enlisted as a counter-terrorist expert during the Kenyan Emergency.[34]

Louis Leakey with *Homo habilis* skull (in his hand), an *Australopithecus* from Pininj, north of Olduvai (in front of his hand) and the skull of a male gorilla (on right)

From coverage of the Mau Mau insurgency in *The Illustrated London News*, 17 January 1953

An important component of the security strategy used to combat Mau Mau was the forced relocation of Kikuyu tribespeople. Another site where, in the Commonwealth at the beginning of 1955, there was conspicuous forced homelessness and dispossession was at Johannesburg in South Africa. Here racist Afrikaans policies of the Department of Native Affairs entailed the 'transfer' of black populations from suburbs like Sophiatown and their relocation to a Government-built project, Meadowlands. There was forced demolition and purification of domestic territory – 'anti-rodent squads moved in with cyanide gas-pumps and demolition squads took over after fumigation was finished. These houses were demolished in order to prevent other families moving in'.[35] This displacement of the Sophiatown residents was widely displayed in the British media and may have been a contributory factor in Kneale's representation of the bulldozing of the English village of Winnerden Flats by Government authorities and the transfer of its inhabitants to a hutted New Town camp.

With such contemporary contexts and with the prominence of dispossession in the narrative of the *Quatermass* trilogy, we can utilise Renee L. Bergland's concept of 'the national uncanny', and relocate it onto British and Commonwealth territory, rather than North American soil. Bergland proposed 'the national uncanny' as a central mode in American fiction arising as an artistic translation – a figuring – of the dispossession of the original inhabitants of the country and their replacement by ghosts which haunted and possessed the new, white subjects of the United States.[36] He has observed that 'Puritan writings described native Americans as demonic manifestations of an internalised psychic struggle. Ever since, spectral Indians have returned to American letters'.[37] This is the terrain of *QP*'s narrative, where demonic Martians are the aggressive, monstrous part of the mental make-up of post-colonial homo sapiens. Quatermass' monsters, his demons and aliens are all migrant, but they are simultaneously rapacious colonists: in *QE* they are homeless in outer space, 'The malignant force that penetrates into the rocket is an immaterial form of life "drifting" in space itself…';[38] in *QII* the aliens are migrants from 'Frozen worlds with atmospheres of poison gas…';[39] while in *QP* the Martians were escaping from a dying planet. In 1954, faced with the likelihood of the extinction of Britons, packed into their urban concentrations under nuclear attack, the Conservative historian Sir Arthur Bryant urged the Prime Minister, Sir Winston Churchill, to disperse the British population from the island. Churchill was asked to contemplate launching 'a crusade for distributing the British people more evenly through the underpopulated areas of the English speaking Commonwealth'.[40]

With Every Race Riot

The news bulletin that is played by Ronay from a radio at the dig on the Knightsbridge building site in *QP* reports the politics and, more especially, the racial politics of a world of the near future that Kneale imagines as structuring the narrative of the serial. This is a world of profound nuclear menace, post-colonial mayhem abroad and racist violence in the Midlands, which is juxtaposed with the news of the discoveries of 'the earliest known hominid'.[41] 'In Vienna, the conference on nuclear disarmament remains deadlocked by failure to agree an agenda. Terrorist activity in Nigeria has been responsible for 87 more deaths during the past month. Police report that Birmingham was peaceful last night after almost a week of racial disturbances'.[42] The imaginary racial disturbances in Birmingham, which are reported in this factualist mode at the beginning of *QP*, caused controversy and a formal protest from leaders of the Birmingham Afro-Caribbean community to the BBC in December 1958. Following the real race riots in Nottingham on the nights of 30 and 31 August 1958, there were racial attacks in Notting Hill, London on 1 and 2 September and it was at this moment that Kneale was devising his screenplay for *QP*. At its worst 'a mob of 2000 youths were attacking coloured people's houses'.[43] The riots seemed to signify a particular irrationality, which was criminal, extreme right-wing and a hangover from imperial and colonial prejudices. And it was this aspect of aggression and violence to racial others which commentators tried to immediately examine: 'Indeed, faced with this madness, the sane everywhere must mobilise … [against] the atavistic urges of the few'.[44]

The thrust of the concluding episode of Kneale's *QP* concentrated on this topic of atavism by the revelation of a racist eugenics practised by the Martians. Kneale's narrative disclosed the reactivation of a repressed loathing and violence to those perceived as 'other', a pattern embedded deeply in the human, all too human, consciousness of the imaginary Londoners who had mounted a pogrom against those genetically different from themselves during the brief night of horror when London reverted to being a Martian colony, just as it had been tens of thousands of years before. Those who carried Martian engineered genes had turned on the remnants of the older Neanderthal race and Quatermass' colleague, Ronay, the Jewish palaeontologist and identifier of Kabbalistic markings on the door to the flight deck of the Martian spaceship. 'Smarter than Quatermass',[45] Ronay manages to resist the racist siren call of the reawakened murderous Martian consciousness. The suggestion here is that this may well be because of his Jewish genetic make-up, one untouched by Martian eugenic surgery at the dawn of *homo sapiens*' existence. Here Kneale himself slipped towards

Coverage of the Notting Hill Riots in
The Illustrated London News, 13 September 1958

ENGLAND'S FIRST RIOTS BETWEEN WHITE AND COLOURED PEOPLE.

ARREST IS MADE (LEFT) DURING THE RIOTING BETWEEN COLOURED AND WHITE PEOPLE WHICH TOOK PLACE IN NOTTING HILL, LONDON, ON SEPTEMBER 1.

A POLICEMAN WITH HIS ALSATIAN POLICE DOG WALKS WITH A GROUP OF WHITE PEOPLE DURING THE NOTTING HILL DISTURBANCES.

YOUTH IS MARCHED AWAY INTO CUSTODY BY TWO POLICEMEN. WAS ONE OF ABOUT THIRTY PEOPLE ARRESTED BEFORE MIDNIGHT ON SEPTEMBER 1 DURING THE NOTTING HILL RIOTING.

ALFRED ROAD, PADDINGTON: A CAN OF BLAZING PETROL WAS HURLED THROUGH THIS WINDOW OF A COLOURED WOMAN'S FLAT.

A WHITE MAN BEING SEARCHED DURING A FURTHER NIGHT OF RIOTING IN THE NOTTING HILL DISTRICT ON SEPTEMBER 2, THE FOURTH SUCCESSIVE NIGHT OF TROUBLE.

GREAT CROWD OF COLOURED PEOPLE LEAVING FRIENDS' HOUSE, EUSTON ROAD, LONDON, LAST DAY, AFTER LISTENING TO AN ADDRESS BY JAMAICA'S CHIEF MINISTER, MR. NORMAN MANLEY.

MR. NORMAN MANLEY TALKING TO BOTH WHITE AND COLOURED PEOPLE IN ST. MARK'S ROAD, NOTTING HILL, WHEN HE TOURED THE AREA LAST SATURDAY.

"I've come here to help. I've not come here to quarrel," said Mr. Norman Manley, Jamaica's Chief Minister, when he arrived in England last Friday to help solve the problems arising out of the grave outbreak of inter-racial rioting which had broken out for the first time in this country. With Manley was Mr. Alan Lennox-Boyd, Colonial Secretary, and Dr. Carl Forbiniere, who is Deputy Prime Minister of the West Indies Federation.

Two days later Dr. Hugh Cummins, Premier of Barbados, also arrived here for discussions. The chief centres of disturbance have been Nottingham and the Notting Hill district of London, where on one evening police reserves had to be called out to cope with a mob of more than 2000 youths who were attacking coloured people's houses. Later the Government announced that there would be "the utmost strictness" in the impartial enforcement of the law.

problematic territory and recalls D.H. Lawrence's enthusiasm for the paintings of the Jewish artist Mark Gertler, in 1916, which were based on his ethnic fantasy that Gertler belonged to an 'older race'. And everywhere, in the wake of the actual and attempted Notting Hill pogrom at the beginning of September 1958, there were more atavistic gestures of separation and purification in the calls, by British Trade Unions and the liberal Left, exemplified by *The Daily Mirror*'s call for an end to immigration from the Commonwealth.[46]

Kneale represented this imagined London pogrom, in *QP*, as a revivification of the ride of the Devil – 'The Wild Hunt' – first performed in archaic ethnic cleansing on the surface of Mars. Electronically transcribed by the mediumistic psychometrics of Ronay's Welsh assistant, this hasty news-footage of massacres is one of the most gothic passages in the series as a whole, like the snatched photographic source of a Bacon horror. In the trials that followed the attempted Notting Hill pogrom, a kind of Wild Hunt was woven into the judicial narrative. Describing a series of homicidal attacks by a white gang on the night of 29 August 1958, Mr Justice Salmon said that the violent rioters were young men who 'set out on a cruel and vicious manhunt'.[47]

Additionally, post-colonial insecurities in Africa and the Middle East were also contexts for some of the anxieties mediated in the epic of *QP*. The violent panicking and murderous mob, seeking out its prey in *QP*, may have had as one point of origin the photographs of street turmoil in the Near and Middle East earlier in 1958. This was a repetition of the dreads of three years earlier, when Pan-Arabism began to remove some of the assurances of any continued British, American and French presences across the Near and Middle East, unhinging western identity by foregrounding an alien insurgency, at the time of *QII*.[48]

In the summer of 1958, the Pan-Arabism of Nassar and the United Arab Republic fomented strife in the Lebanon, and a Ba'athist revolt in Iraq, led by Abdel Karim Kaseem, on 14 July destroyed and murdered the monarchy of the British-sponsored King Faisal. It was the aspect of a violent street revolution which provided a spectacle of terror, of uncovered foreigners and political enemies torn to pieces on Baghdad streets, as *The Illustrated London News* reported in, 'The Horror of Revolution: Street Mobs Uncontrolled and Bent on Destruction of Life and Property'.[49] This actual mayhem and the grim home-grown scenes of the Notting Hill riots was mirrored, as Quatermass says, in the set piece savageries on the imaginary streets of Knightsbridge at the climax of *QP*. To preserve their colony the Martians will '…kill every mutation away from the set pattern! Destroy all that didn't belong to it – every living creature…'.[50] In an epic contemporary science fiction myth, Kneale condensed the atrocities of July, in Baghdad, the August/September race riots of London and the arrival of the Thor nuclear missiles in the same month in an allegorised form as the release of ancient evils from Mars genetically implanted in the human psyche. Quatermass' final baleful warning at the close of *QP*, his warning of genocidal and racist urges, was also the object of censorship attempts within the BBC:[51] 'Every war, crisis, witch-hunt, race riot and purge, is a reminder and warning. We are the Martians. If we cannot control the inheritance within us, this will be the second dead planet.'[52] But viewed in another perspective, Kneale's and Quatermass' fears were of the same *kultur pessimismus* stamp as those of Viscount Samuel, who wrote 'Man in the Cosmos' in 1958: '…the daily catalogue in the newspapers – reported in an instant from every quarter of the globe – of riots, revolts and outrages … all this casts over our civilisation a dark flood of pessimism … One of our leading historians, G.M. Trevelyan speaks of this era as "the fall of European civilisation"'.[53] The *Quatermass* trilogy speaks to, and partakes of, this cultural pessimism in that epoch of de-colonisation.

Notes

1. cf. 'I think I'm going mad', Nigel Kneale, *Quatermass II*, Harmondsworth: Penguin, 1960, p.37. Critical writing on the *Quatermass* trilogy is sparse. The most imaginative is the first, David Sylvester's 1956 account, in terms of comparisons with art and visual culture: 'The Anglicisation of Outer Space', cf. note 15.
2. M. Heidegger, 'The Question Concerning Technology', trans. William Lovitt, *The Question Concerning Technology and Other Essays*, New York, NY: Harper & Row, 1977, pp 3–35, p.16.
3. cf. Jonathan Norton Leonard's characterisation of Von Braun in *Flight into Space*, London: Pan, 1956, p.53: 'something of a prophet and something of a mystic … he worries and frightens them (i.e. fellow scientists) with his technological visions'.
4. 'Our £100,000,000 Atom Stake', *Picture Post*, 7 December 1946, pp 9–10, 37.
5. cf. D.A. Mellor, *The Neo-Romantic Imagination in Britain, 1935–1955*, London: Barbican Art Gallery, 1987.
6. Andrew Pixley, *Viewing Notes/Quatermass*, BBC DVD, 2005, p.28.
7. Richard Levin, *Television by Design*, London: Bodley Head, 1961, p.94.
8. Anon, *The London Planetarium*, c.1957, p.7.
9. ibid., p.48.
10. ibid., p.17.
11. ibid., p.16.
12. Nigel Kneale, *Quatermass and the Pit*, Harmondsworth: Penguin, 1961, p.11.
13. Lynne Cooke in N. Serota and S. Nairne (eds), *British Sculpture in the 20th Century*, London: Whitechapel Art Gallery, 1981, p.169.
14. J. Epstein, *Autobiography*, London: Art Treasures Book Club, 1963, p.56.
15. David Sylvester, 'The Anglicisation of Outer Space', *Encounter*, vol.X, no.1, January 1956, pp 69–72, p.69.
16. ibid., p.71.
17. cf. B. Clarke, *Four Minutes Warning*, Stroud: Tempus, 2005, pp 14–16.
18. Nigel Kneale, *Quatermass II*, op. cit., p.117.
19. A. Pixley, op. cit., p.13.
20. Joseph Conrad, *Heart of Darkness*, Harmondsworth: Penguin, 2000, p.32.
21. ibid.
22. Conclusion to Arthur C. Clarke, 'Pioneers in Space Suits', *Picture Post*, 26 July 1952, pp 39, 41.
23. 'Blueprint of a Dream/Liner to Mars', *Picture Post*, 1 March 1952, pp 24–25 and p.57; 'Pioneers in Space Suits', *Picture Post*, 26 July 1952, pp 39, 41.
24. T.A. Heppenheimer, *Countdown/A History of Space Flight*, New York, NY: John Wiley & Sons, 1997, p.179.
25. 'Dan Dare Recalled', *Picture Post*, 29 September 1951, p.3.
26. cf. Jonathan Norton Leonard, *Flight into Space*, London: Pan, 1956, pp 67–68.
27. Ritchie Calder, 'Moon Hazards', *The New Statesman*, 23 August 1958, p.214.
28. Joseph Conrad, op. cit., p.33.
29. Nigel Kneale in conversation with the author, 9 July 2006.
30. Nigel Kneale, *Quatermass and the Pit*, op. cit., p.13.
31. Dr L.S.B. Leakey, 'Olduvai: Light on Chellean Man's Way of Life …', *The Illustrated London News*, 5 July 1958, p.41.
32. 'Air and Ground Patrols and the Mau Mau threat to the Settler', *The Illustrated London News*, 17 January 1953, p.253 and cf. Ian McDougall, 'The Battle against Mau Mau', *The Listener*, 16 August 1953, pp 85–86. For two recent accounts of the Kenyan Emergency see D. Anderson, *Histories of the Hanged*, London: Weidenfeld & Nicholson, 2005, and C. Elkins, *Imperial Reckoning: The Untold Story of Britain's Gulag in Kenya*, New York, NY: Henry Holt, 2005.
33. P.V. Tobias, 'White African: An Appreciation and some personal memories of Louis Leakey' in G.Ll. Isaac and E.R. McCown (eds), *Human Origins/Louis Leakey and the East African Evidence*, Menlo Park, CA: W.A. Benjamin, p.56.
34. cf. G.Ll. Isaac and E.R. McCown (eds), ibid., p.61.
35. 'Sophiatown and Meadowlands: Two Facets of the Transfer of Johannesburg's Africans', *The Illustrated London News*, 19 February 1955, pp 314–15.
36. Renee L. Bergland, *The National Uncanny*, Hanover, NH: University Press of New England, 2000.
37. ibid., p.1.
38. David Sylvester, 'The Anglicisation of Outer Space', *Encounter*, vol.X, no.1, pp.69–72, p.71.
39. Nigel Kneale, *Quatermass II*, op. cit., p.91.
40. Sir Arthur Bryant, 'Our Notebook', *The Illustrated London News*, 14 August 1954, p.242.
41. Nigel Kneale, *Quatermass and the Pit*, op. cit., p.27.
42. ibid.
43. 'England's first Riots Between White and Coloured People', *The Illustrated London News*, 13 September 1958, p.415.
44. 'The Hooligans of Notting Hill', *The New Statesman*, 6 September 1958, p.261.
45. Nigel Kneale in conversation with the author, 9 July 2006.
46. Francis Williams, 'Fleet Street', *The New Statesman*, 6 September 1958, p.265.
47. Dan Jacobson, 'After Notting Hill', *Encounter*, December 1958, pp 3–10, p.9.
48. cf. Sir Stephen King-Hall, 'The Crisis in the Middle East', *The Listener*, 20 October 1955, pp 636–38.
49. *The Illustrated London News*, 2 August 1958, pp 188–89.
50. Nigel Kneale, *Quatermass and the Pit*, op. cit., p.188.
51. Nigel Kneale in conversation with the author, 9 July 2006.
52. Nigel Kneale, *Quatermass and the Pit*, op. cit., p.188.
53. Viscount Samuel, 'Man in the Cosmos', *The Listener*, 25 December 1958, pp 1059–60.

'TIME WAS ON THE TRIFFIDS' SIDE. THEY HAD ONLY TO GO ON WAITING WHILE WE USED UP OUR RESOURCES. FIRST THE FUEL, THEN NO MORE WIRE TO MEND THE FENCES. AND THEY OR THEIR DESCENDANTS WOULD STILL BE WAITING THERE WHEN THE WIRE RUSTED THROUGH...'

JOHN WYNDHAM, *THE DAY OF THE TRIFFIDS*
(MICHAEL JOSEPH, LONDON, 1951)

LOOK OUT... IT'S

THE THING

from another world !

HOWARD HAWKS' *Astounding* MOVIE

SPACE ODYSSEY:

A JOURNEY WITH OTHERS

BY **CYLENA SIMONDS**

Far from strangers, race and science fiction have been travel companions throughout the long history of human social interaction. In fact, you could say that the concept of race as a biological determination is itself a persuasive work of science fiction. Intrigued, but don't know where to begin your journey? Fear not. Join us on an annotated tour of the best and worst films, TV series, and writing, evoking race as an alien spectre. Adventurers beware: this list may contain spoilers!

THE WAR OF THE WORLDS
(RADIO BROADCAST), 1938, PROD. ORSON WELLES
Based on the novel by H.G. Wells, the genius of Welles' broadcast was to re-present the story as a series of emergency news broadcasts, interspersed with regular features of radio programming such as weather reports and recorded music. So convinced were listeners that hundreds of people called the police and fled their homes in teror. Commentators have since speculated that concurrent news of World War I in Europe, which was also terrifyingly close to home, difficult to fathom but unbearably real, made Welles' blurring of fact and fiction credible to American audiences.

THE DAY THE EARTH STOOD STILL
(20TH CENTURY FOX, USA), 1951, DIR. ROBERT WISE
The inspiration for many contemporary artists featured in the *Alien Nation* exhibition, the premise of this film stands miles apart from the other films of this period. After the end of World War II and the discovery of nuclear fission, an alien tells the

people of Earth that we must live peacefully or be destroyed as a danger to other planets. As occurs all too often in our present day, soldiers responded by immediately shooting the visitor and asking questions later. Whereas many of the films of the 1950s justify the fear of Communist threat, this film explicitly critiques the paranoia and fear of difference and issues a prophetic warning against substituting fear for reason.

Quatermass II: Enemy from Space / Terre contre Satellite, 1957, original French film poster

THE THING
(RKO RADIO PICTURES / WINCHESTER FILMS, USA), 1951, DIR. CHRISTIAN NYBY AND HOWARD HAWKS
A US army squadron based at the North Pole, protecting secret science experiments from the Russians, stumbles across a crashed alien ship. Featuring detailed descriptions of high-tech scientific gadgets and long scenes discussing security procedures, the film attempts to reassure the audience that the World Wars have prepared humans to address any kind of threat. So who, after conquering the Nazis, would be man's most formidable foe? A giant Frankenstein-double who is actually a super-intelligent vampiric vegetable!

INVADERS FROM MARS
(20TH CENTURY FOX, USA), 1953, DIR. WILLIAM CAMERON MENZIES
Adolescent David is the first and only witness to the landing of an alien ship, but his parents believe it's just a nightmare. Nevertheless, his father agrees to investigate, but when he returns he has a radically changed personality. When his mother and the sheriff also become victims, the young boy is able to convince the local doctor and astronomer. They call in the US Army, but in the end it is David who saves the planet by turning the aliens' weapons against them.

IT CAME FROM OUTER SPACE
(UNIVERSAL, USA), 1953, DIR. JACK ARNOLD
A variation on the theme of a stranger hidden among us, in this account hideous alien beings clone two of the inhabitants of a small Arizona town in order to pass unnoticed while they gather supplies to fix their ship. Although the aliens seem peaceful and only wish to return to their home, the sheriff insists on violently attacking them before they make any moves, in spite of the local astronomer's pleas for patience and tolerance. Most striking in the film are the beautiful scenes of the desert, which is often commented upon as an alien and hostile environment.

It Came from Outer Space, 1953, original US film poster

THE QUATERMASS EXPERIMENT
(BBC PRODUCTIONS, TV SERIES, UK), 1953, WRITTEN BY NIGEL KNEALE, DIR. RUDOLF CARTIER
QUATERMASS II
(BBC TV SERIES, UK), 1955, WRITTEN BY NIGEL KNEALE, DIR. RUDOLPH CARTIER
QUATERMASS AND THE PIT
(BBC TV SERIES, UK), 1958, WRITTEN BY NIGEL KNEALE, DIR. RUDOLPH CARTIER
As terrifying today as when it was first broadcast, the recently re-mastered BBC TV serials chronicled the adventures of rocket scientist Professor Bernard Quatermass. Succeeding in its dramatic tension to such an extent that the BBC felt the need to forewarn viewers 'who may have a nervous disposition', the series pioneered the concept that alien threats may be invisible and hidden among the population – a narrative device that would later become a feature of the genre. In an original climactic twist, the final series, *Quatermass and the Pit*, takes these speculations a step further by proposing that we, the inhabitants of Earth, are all the results of alien modification, thus the fear of the other is revealed to be fear of otherness within ourselves.

THE WAR OF THE WORLDS
(PARAMOUNT, USA), 1953, DIR. BYRON HASKIN
Explicitly referencing World Wars I and II in the script, this first film adaptation of H.G. Wells' novel conveys the widespread paranoia of the 'Red

FILM PROD. ANGIELSKIEJ
REŻYSERIA: VAL GUEST

ZEMSTA KOSMOSU

WYKONAWCY: MARGIA DEAN · JACK WARNER · BRIAN DONLEVY i inni

Menace' in the US during the McCarthy era. The Martians are invulnerable to the latest defence weapons, even the atomic bomb, and all seems to be hopeless. Yet the human race is saved due to the aliens' vulnerability to Earth's common bacteria, a fact credited to God's divine plan.

THIS ISLAND EARTH
(UNIVERSAL, USA), 1955,
DIR. JACK ARNOLD AND JOSEPH NEWMAN

When a secret alien science laboratory on earth is accidentally destroyed, Earth scientists are abducted to the planet Metaluna to provide atomic power to protect the Metalunans from their enemies, the Zagons. When the Earth scientists arrive, the Metalunans are not only losing their battle against the Zagons, but are also under threat internally, as their own insect servant class has taken this opportunity to revolt against their oppressive masters.

FORBIDDEN PLANET
(MGM, USA), 1956, DIR. FRED WILCOX

A rescue team finds only two survivors on the planet Altair IV, Dr Edward Morbius and his nubile daughter Altara, who are mysteriously flourishing on their own among incredible resources and advanced technology – that is, until an enormous invisible monster begins to attack. Invulnerable and extremely violent, it soon becomes clear that the monster is a result of the doctor's secret experiments with the native aliens' equipment, which has unleashed a material manifestation of his Id. Forced literally to confront his own demon, the doctor sacrifices himself to save his daughter.

INVASION OF THE BODY SNATCHERS
(ALLIED ARTISTS, USA), 1956, DIR. DON SIEGEL

Once again, the enemy is one of us. These aliens appear identical to the individuals they replace save for subtle changes in personality and behaviour. Aligned to a mysterious purpose that remains unexplained, the impostors cannot be negotiated with or reasoned out of conflict and as such suggest that the persuasiveness of Communist ideology can only be challenged through aggression. Most prescient is the way the film almost forewarns of current US and British anxieties about how we distinguish between 'us' and 'them' when visual signifiers of difference are unreliable.

I MARRIED A MONSTER FROM OUTER SPACE
(PARAMOUNT, USA), 1958, DIR. JEAN FOWLER JR

Aliens from outer space are slowly switching places with humans – one of the first being a young man about to get married. Is he the quiet sensitive type, preferring to stay at home rather than meet his mates at the pub? Beware: he may not be a harmless metro-sexual but a creature from outer space! The aliens have been sent to earth to breed with human women, and this film evokes the period's unacknowledged but prevalent fear of interracial relationships, particularly in the horrifying scene where the 'real' men hunt down the alien boyfriends with dogs.

VILLAGE OF THE DAMNED
(MGM, UK), 1960, DIR. WOLF RILLA

In a small quiet town in England all the women become mysteriously pregnant, even the grannies. The children are almost identical when born and, although they all have blond hair and blue eyes, the allusion to contaminated births clearly echoes concurrent fears of miscegenation. But its not just the way they look that makes the children strange, they also have mysterious telepathic powers that allow them to know each other's thoughts and to control anyone who opposes them. By depicting the bond between the children as unnatural, the film evokes Cold War demonisations of the Communist 'one-mind' where the welfare of the group is held to be more important than the individual. The film is based on the novel *The Midwich Cuckoos* by John Wyndham (Michael Joseph, London, 1957).

THE DAY OF THE TRIFFIDS
(ALLIED ARTISTS, UK), 1963, DIR. STEVE SEKELY

Two competing anxieties crowd the plot of this film: the natural disaster of a meteor shower that renders most humans blind, and the giant triffids, homicidal ambulatory plants that arrived via the same rock. Our protagonists drive through Europe collecting unafflicted allies to fight the invaders, in a romantic idealisation of a united Europe overcoming any challenge. When the triffids are found to be easily dispatched by dousing with sea-water, the film leaves open a disturbing misconception that madness and chaos would naturally follow disability. Based on the novel *The Day of the Triffids* by John Wyndham (Michael Joseph, London, 1951).

BABEL-17
(ACE BOOKS, USA), 1966, SAMUEL DELANY

In this early work by seminal African American sci-fi author Delany, who is renowned for addressing sexuality and racial difference, language is a formidable weapon used by alien invaders and a poet is recruited as the humans' only hope for survival. Never an easy read, the more ambitious should tackle the self-reflexive semiotic exploration *Dhalgren*, his most critically acclaimed and most challenging novel. It is also worth looking out for his non-fiction writing on the political and social value of science fiction.

STAR TREK
(DESILU PRODUCTIONS, TV SERIES, USA) 1966–69, CREATED BY GENE RODDENBERRY

This television series was progressive in its time for positing that the future of space exploration would necessarily occur in tandem with Earth's resolution of conflicts between humans on the basis of race or national borders. The series features the first fictional African American astronaut, Uhura, played by actor Nichelle Nichols, whose ground-breaking role inspired generations of black scientists and sci-fi writers. Such was the series commitment to an idealised future that Capt. Kirk and Lt Uhura challenged audiences with the first ever interracial kiss to appear on television.

PLANET OF THE APES
(20TH CENTURY FOX, USA), 1968, DIR. FRANKLIN J. SCHAFFNER

Although lacking in subtlety at times, this camp endeavour drives home its message of the injustice of racial inequality in a humorous and enjoyable manner. Apes have evolved to be the dominant species and subject humans to medical experiments, slave labour, forced breeding and other inhumane acts, similar to those perpetuated against African slaves since they were first brought to the US in the 18th century. The compassion and open-mindedness of a few apes (read abolitionists) lead to the escape of the hero but the film disappoints by leaving the racist and unjust structure of ape society unchallenged. A shocking inter-species kiss between a female ape and the male protagonist lead to public outrage at the time.

THX 1138
(AMERICAN ZOETROPE, USA), 1970, DIR. GEORGE LUCAS

Visually striking, Lucas uses a palette of stark overwhelming 'whiteness' to convey the oppressive control of individuality in his dystopic future society. Not only are all of the actors (save one) Caucasian, but also the clothing and environment are endlessly and starkly white, without shadows or embellishments. The towering Don Pedro Colley plays the society's only black inhabitant and he isn't 'real', he's a hologram!

THE MAN WHO FELL TO EARTH
(BRITISH LION FILM CORPORATION, UK), 1976, DIR. NICHOLAS ROEG

This stylised and visually rich film was David Bowie's mainstream cinema debut. The plot is an immigration allegory, where Earth offers the promise of hope and salvation from starvation and dehydration in Bowie's arid desert home planet. In a reversal of typical alien narrative, his efforts to find solutions in the Promised Land are futile and the protagonist cannot even convince his hosts that he is an alien.

BROTHER FROM ANOTHER PLANET
(A-TRAIN FILMS, USA), 1984, DIR. JOHN SAYLES

This is a modern day fable set in the present where the brother from the title is an alien (resembling a mute black man) who escapes persecution on his home planet, crash lands in the Hudson River and finds himself in Harlem. Surprisingly light-hearted and humorous in parts, the film still manages to evoke subtle anxieties and melancholy in its allegories of escape from immigration and slavery in southern USA.

DAWN
(WARNER BOOKS, INC., USA), 1987, OCTAVIA BUTLER

Aliens attempt to colonise Earth after a nuclear war has destroyed most of the planet and humanity risks extinction. They offer the surviving humans an opportunity to survive, if they accept the aliens' complex proposal of sexual integration into the family unit. Concerned with the legacy of colonialism and the acceptance of difference, Butler's stories are imbued with a pathos that resonates uncannily with present-day concerns. Also see her excellent futuristic political series, *Parable of the Sower*.

ALIEN NATION
(20TH CENTURY FOX, USA), 1988, DIR. GRAHAM PARKER

This sci-fi spin on the ubiquitous cop buddy film depicts a reluctant officer teamed with a 'newcomer' from an alien race that has immigrated to Earth. The film is disturbingly poignant for how it reveals the casual everyday racism faced by immigrants, despite the fact that it does this by trotting out weary stereotypes, such the hyper-sexuality of the female of the species.

FUTURE EARTHS: UNDER AFRICAN SKIES
(PENGUIN), 1993, ED. MIKE RESNIK

This is a collection of short stories, featuring contributions from sci-fi gurus Kim Stanley Robinson and Bruce Sterling, set in an alternate or future continent of Africa. It is interesting for its pervasive fantasies of 'Mother Africa' that afflict the writers, who cannot seem to help but evoke the stereotypical mythologies in their visions.

THE ARRIVAL
(LIVE ENTERTAINMENT, MEDIAWORKS INC.
AND STEELWORK FILMS, USA), 1996, DIR. DAVID TWOHY

Shocking for all the wrong reasons, this film starring Charlie Sheen boasts insufferable writing and acting along with its blatantly racist premise: Mexicans are actually reptilian aliens infiltrating the US through loose immigration policies and plotting to take over the world by changing the climate so that it becomes unbearably hot! Released during high profile media coverage of US companies exploiting cheap labour across the border, while the government attempted to refuse to recognise the human rights of illegal workers within the US, this film would have been an incitement to riot if it were not so preposterous.

MEN IN BLACK
(AMBLIN ENTERTAINMENT, COLUMBIA PICTURES CORPORATION,
MACDONALD/PARKES PRODUCTION, USA), 1997,
DIR. BARRY SONNENFELD

Eschewing any subtlety in its racial metaphors, the film proposes that a secret alien immigration programme has been successfully assimilating visitors from other worlds into the US for decades (successful, that is, until giant roach aliens arrive and spoil everything).

STARSHIP TROOPERS
(TOUCHSTONE PICTURES, USA), 1997,
DIR. PAUL VERHOEVEN

In a terrifying future where citizenship is only granted to those who serve in the military, this ambivalent satire follows a group of young teenagers who eagerly join the Earth's long war against the inhabitants (all forms of giant bugs) of Klendathu. While the teens buy into the media propaganda that depicts the bugs as mindless violent fiends, the film slowly reveals contradictory evidence that the aliens are only defending their planet from aggression initiated by Earth in order to steal Klendathu's natural resources. Although many viewers read the film as a poignant dramatisation of how fascism seduces the population, the most disturbing success of its message is that the film inspired the US military to set up recruitment booths outside some regional cinemas when it was released.

BLUE LIGHT
(LITTLE, BROWN AND CO., USA), 1998, WALTER MOSELY

A mysterious extra-terrestrial intelligence passes through California leading to the enlightenment of a few individuals and initiating profound changes for human society. More known for his crime novels, Mosely has been a vocal champion of the ability of science fiction to raise political and social debates. See also *Futureland* (1999) for dystopic developments that raise questions of social and political responsibility.

DARK MATTER: A CENTURY OF SPECULATIVE FICTION FROM THE AFRICAN DIASPORA
(TIME WARNER INTL, USA), 2000, ED. SHEREE R. THOMAS

A must-have collection of short stories that contextualises fictional writing by black authors in literary traditions from the Harlem Renaissance to the present. Including little known texts by Amiri Baraka and Ishmael Reed, as well as works by Samuel Delany and Octavia Butler, the authors explore the fantastic and futuristic through alternative histories and alien encounters.

SO LONG BEEN DREAMING: POSTCOLONIAL SCIENCE FICTION
(ARSENAL PULP PRESS, CANADA), 2004, ED. NALO HOPKINSON

An impressive collection of stories by writers of Aboriginal, African, East and South Asian diasporas exploring the ramifications of colonialism in outer space informed by post-colonial cultural theory. Especially valuable is the range of female First Nations writers such as Celu Amberstone, Larissa Lai and Eden Robinson among others whose visions of home, belonging and hospitality in alien worlds resonate with lessons still to be learned.

FURTHER ADVENTURES

ACADEMIC ANALYSES

Elisabeth Anne Leonard, *Into Darkness Peering: Race and Color in the Fantastic (Contributions to the Study of Science Fiction & Fantasy)*, USA: Greenwood Press, 1997.

Sandra M. Grayson, *Visions of the Third Millennium: Black Science Fiction Novelists Write the Future*, USA: Africa Research and Publications, 2002.

De Witt Douglas Kilgore, *Astrofuturism: Science Race and Visions of Utopia in Space*, USA: University of Pennsylvania Press, 2003.

Laura Chernaik, *Social and Virtual Space: Science Fiction, Transnationalism, and the American New Right*, USA: Fairleigh Dickinson University Press, 2005.

Wong Kin Yuen (ed.), *World Weavers: Globalization, Science Fiction, and the Cybernetic Revolution*, China: Hong Kong University Press, 2006.

COMMUNITIES

AFROFUTURISM

A forum and resource that explores futurist themes in black cultural production with extensive references to film, music and literature.
http://www.afrofuturism.net/

CARL BRANDON SOCIETY

An organisation set up to support science fiction written by people of colour, with awards, scholarships, blogs and events calendar.
http://www.carlbrandon.org/

This Island, Earth, 1955, original US film poster

'WHAT WE DON'T UNDERSTAND, WE WANT TO DESTROY.'

JACK ARNOLD, DIR. *IT CAME FROM OUTER SPACE*
(UNIVERSAL, USA, 1953)

BEWARE THE EYES THAT PARALYZE !!!

CHILDREN OF THE DAMNED

it's all new! from M·G·M

OUTER SPACE

ARTISTS IN ALIEN NATION

LAYLAH ALI

Laylah Ali was born in Buffalo, New York, in 1968. Working primarily in painting and drawing, Ali creates cartoonish figures that play out enigmatic narratives or stand in isolation, their simplicity belying darker stories of ethnicity, difference and African American history. Ali completed her BA at Williams College, Williamstown (1991) after which she attended the Whitney Museum Independent Study Program, New York (1991–92), Skowhegan School of Painting and Sculpture, Maine (1993) and Washington University, St Louis (1994) where she received her MFA. Ali has had a number of solo exhibitions, including at the Gertrude Contemporary Art Spaces, Melbourne (2005), Contemporary Art Museum St Louis, St Louis (2004), Albright-Knox Art Gallery, Buffalo (2003), Atlanta College of Art Gallery, Atlanta (2002) and the Museum of Contemporary Art, Chicago (1999). Ali's work has featured in many group exhibitions including the *Whitney Biennial*, Whitney Museum of American Art, New York (2004), *Street-Smart Art: Five Artists to Create Billboards*, Walker Art Center, Minneapolis (2004), *me & more*, Kunstmuseum, Lucerne (2003), *Fault Lines: Contemporary African Art and Shifting Landscapes*, 50th International Art Exhibition, La Biennale di Venezia, Venice (2003) and *Splat Boom Pow! The Influence of Comics in Contemporary Art*, Contemporary Arts Museum, Houston (2003). For *Projects 75* at the Museum of Modern Art, New York, Ali created an artist's book (2002). In 2001, Ali was awarded the Premio Regione Piemonte 2001 from the Fondazione Sandretto Re Rebaudengo, Turin, and in 2000 the ICA Artist Prize, Institute of Contemporary Art, Boston. Ali lives and works in Massachusetts.

HAMAD BUTT

Hamad Butt was born in Lahore in 1962 and graduated from Goldsmiths College, London (1990). In 1994 he died of an AIDS-related illness. Through his installation-based practice, Butt investigated notions of pure science, from complex calculations on the triple point of iodine to experimentations with holograms. During his brief career, he was the subject of solo exhibitions at John Hansard Gallery, Southampton (1992) and Milch Gallery, London (1990) and featured in the major group exhibition *Rites of Passage*, Tate Gallery, London (1995). Following his death, his work has featured in a number of group exhibitions including *zerozerozero*, Whitechapel Art Gallery, London (1999) and *Current Research*, Millais Gallery, Southampton (1998). The artist's book *Familiars*, in effect Butt's final project, was published posthumously in 1996 according to his instructions.

EDGAR CLEIJNE

Edgar Cleijne was born in Eindhoven in 1963 and graduated from the Rotterdam Conservatory (1990). As a photographer and filmmaker he focuses on large-scale interventions in the urban landscape enforced by negotiations between the individual and the state. Concentrating on the individual choices that result in complex urban developments, Cleijne portrays the struggle to live and be represented within systems of official denial. He has exhibited his work in *Spectacular City: Photographing the Future*, Netherlands Architecture Institute, Rotterdam and NRW Forum – Kultur und Wirtschaft, Düsseldorf (2006), *Migration and Development*, Museo Nacional, San Jose, Costa Rica (2006), *Greenspace*, Valencia (2005), *Lisbon*

Photo Biennial, Lisbon (2003), *Fotodocs*, Museum Boijmans van Beuningen, Rotterdam (2002), *Mutations*, arc en rêve centre d'architecture, Bordeaux (2002–03, travelling) and *City Vision, Media-City*, Seoul (2000). In 2001 he started a collaboration with the architect Rem Koolhaas on *The Harvard Design School Project on the City – Lagos*, and the subsequent book, *Lagos How It Works*, is due to be published early in 2007. In 2003 he made the film *Lagos Live*, with director and screenwriter Bregtje van der Haak. Cleijne also frequently collaborates with the artist Ellen Gallagher. Their 16mm film pieces have been shown at the Walker Art Center, Minneapolis (2006), Freud Museum, London (2005), Museum of Contemporary Art, North Miami (2005), Fruitmarket Gallery, Edinburgh (2004–05), Henry Art Gallery, University of Washington, Washington (2004) and the Studio Museum, Harlem. Cleijne lives and works in New York and Rotterdam.

ELLEN GALLAGHER

Ellen Gallagher was born in Providence, Rhode Island, in 1965, and studied at Oberlin College, Ohio (1982–84). She completed her painting studies at the School of the Museum of Fine Arts, Boston (1992), where she was the recipient of a Travelling Scholar's Award (1993). In 1993, Gallagher received the Agnes Gund Fellowship to study at the Skowhegan School of Painting and Sculpture, Maine. Through her practice – paintings, drawings, printmaking and film – Gallagher manipulates archival material and popular cultural sources to examine notions of race and identity, although she is equally interested in the formal aspects of her process, the materials, forms, mark making, repetition and rhythm through which she negotiates the relationship between abstraction and representation, the organic and the structured, the personal and the collective. Gallagher has exhibited widely, most recently with solo exhibitions at the Whitney Museum of American Art, New York (2005), Freud Museum, London (2005), Museum of Contemporary Art, North Miami (2005), Fruitmarket Gallery, Edinburgh (2004), Saint Louis Art Museum, St Louis (2003) and the Institute of Contemporary Art, Boston (2001). She has also participated in numerous group exhibitions over her career, including *Heart of Darkness: Kai Althof, Ellen Gallagher/Edgar Cleijne, Thomas Hirshhorn*, Walker Art Center, Minneapolis (2006), *Infinite Painting: Contemporary Painting and Global Realism*, Villa Manin Centre for Contemporary Art, Udine (2006), *Black Panther Rank and File*, Yerba Buena Center for the Arts, San Francisco (2006), *Skin Is a Language*,

Whitney Museum of American Art, New York (2006), *The Fluidity of Time: Selections from the MCA Collection*, Museum of Contemporary Art, Chicago (2005–06), *SITE Santa Fe Fifth International Biennial*, Sante Fe (2004), *Dreams and Conflicts: The Dictatorship of the Viewer*, 50th International Art Exhibition, La Biennale di Venezia, Venice (2003), *Greater New York: New Art in New York Now*, P.S.1. Contemporary Art Center, New York (2000), *Corps (Social)*, Ecole Nationale Supériere des Beaux-Arts, Paris (1999), *Projects*, Irish Museum of Modern Art, Dublin (1997) and the *Whitney Biennal*, Whitney Museum of American Art, New York (1995). In 2000, she was awarded an American Academy Award in Art. She lives and works in New York and Rotterdam.

DAVID HUFFMAN

David Huffman was born in Berkeley, California, in 1963. He received his MFA at the California College of Arts and Crafts, Oakland in 1999, and is now a member of the faculty at the California College of the Arts, San Francisco. Informed by historical and contemporary events, Huffman unfolds an epic story of African American space explorers called Traumasmiles, a civilisation marked by the mask of the minstrel's broad smile, whose metaphoric conflicts parallel nation/state, religious, racial and personal tragedies. Huffman's work has been included in a number of group exhibitions in the United States, including *Black Belt* (2003–04) and *Freestyle* (2001) both held at the Studio Museum in Harlem, New York and the Santa Monica Museum of Art, Santa Monica, *un(Common) Ground: Introductions South*, San Jose Institute of Contemporary Art, San Jose (2002), *Retrofuturist*, New Langton Arts, San Francisco (2001), *Hybrid*, Southern Exposure, San Francisco (2000) and *Bay Area Now 2*, Yerba Buena Center for the Arts, San Francisco (1999–2000). His first major solo exhibition, *Dark Matter: The Art of David Huffman*, was held at the de Saisset Museum, Santa Clara (2004). Huffman is the recipient of the 2005 Artadia Foundation Award. He lives and works in the San Francisco Bay Area.

HEW LOCKE

Hew Locke was born in Edinburgh in 1959 and spent the early part of his life in Georgetown, Guyana (1966–80). He completed his BA at Falmouth School of Art, Falmouth (1988) and his MA in Sculpture at the Royal College of Art, London (1994). In recent years Locke has focused on his fascination and ambivalence around ideas and images of Britishness in a global context, such as the royal family. He explores global cultural fusions, creating complex sculptural collages comprised of an eclectic range of objects, including market-stall mass-produced toys, souvenirs and consumer detritus. Solo exhibitions have taken place at the New Art Gallery, Walsall (2005), Tate Britain, London (2004), Atlanta Contemporary Art Center, Atlanta (2004, travelling), Horniman Museum, London (2002), Chisenhale Gallery, London (2002) and the Victoria and Albert Museum, London (2000). Locke's work has featured in many group exhibitions within the UK, including the *British Art Show 6*, BALTIC Centre for Contemporary Art, Gateshead (2006, travelling), *Boys Who Sew*, Crafts Council, London (2004–05, travelling), *Somewhere – places of refuge in art and life*, Angel Row Gallery, Nottingham (2002, travelling) and *East International*, Norwich Art Gallery, Norwich (2000). In 2000 he received both the Paul Hamlyn Award and the East International Award. Locke lives and works in London.

MAREPE

Marepe was born Marcos Ruis Peixoto in San Antonia de Jesus, Bahia, in 1970 where he still lives and works. The culture of this region, Bahia's traditions and customs, as well as its materials, inform Marepe's conceptual sculptural practice, whether by changing the function and status of common objects or the meaning of local street performances, to create lyrical gestures out of everyday life. His first major solo exhibition was held at the Centre Pompidou, Paris (2005–06) and in 2004 he presented a *Special Project* at P.S.1 in collaboration with the Museum of Modern Art, New York. Since the 1990s Marepe has exhibited widely in international group exhibitions, including *Tropicália: A Revolution in Brazilian Culture*, Museum of Contemporary Art, Chicago (2005–06), travelling), *Poetic Justice*, 8th International Istanbul Biennial, Istanbul (2003), *Dreams and Conflicts: The Dictatorship of the Viewer*, 50th International Art Exhibition, La Biennale di Venezia, Venice (2003), *How Latitudes Become Form: Art in a Global Age*, Walker Art Center, Minneapolis (2003, travelling), *Metropolitan Iconographies*, XXV Bienal de São Paulo, São Paulo (2001) and *The Thread Unraveled: Contemporary Brazilian Art*, El Museo Del Barrio, New York (2001).

HENNA NADEEM

Henna Nadeem was born in Leeds in 1966 and graduated with a MA from the Royal College of Art, London (1993). In Nadeem's complex photographic collages, she superimposes decorative patterns inspired by Islamic, Japanese and Moorish sources onto a wide range of found landscape images, from tourist shots of Africa to chocolate box depictions of 1950s England, integrating disparate visual references to create new cultural readings. Nadeem's recent solo exhibitions include Charleston Farmhouse, as part of *Brighton Photo Biennial* (2006) and the Newlyn Art Gallery, Penzance (2005). Other solo projects include *Henna Nadeem: Picture Book of Britain*, a publication by Photoworks (2006), *trees water rocks* for Piccadilly Circus Underground Station, London (2004–05) and *Billy Bragg*, a billboard commission for Project Gallery, Dublin (2004). She has exhibited widely in group exhibitions across the UK, including *Another Product*, Cornerhouse, Manchester (2006), *Picture of Britain*, Tate Britain (2005), *I want! I want!*, Northern Gallery of Contemporary Art, Sunderland (2003–04, travelling), *Landscape Trauma in the Age of Scopophilia*, Leeds Metropolitan University Gallery (2001–02, travelling), *re:creation; re:construction,* Pump House Gallery, London (2001) and *A Different Kind of Show*, Whitechapel Art Gallery, London (2000). Nadeem has undertaken residencies at the London Print Studio (2004–05), the University of Sunderland in conjunction with Autograph (2003–04), and Camden Arts Centre, London (1997). In 2006, Nadeem was nominated for the Paul Hamlyn Award. She lives and works in London.

KORI NEWKIRK

Kori Newkirk was born in the Bronx, New York, in 1970, and received his BFA from the School of the Art Institute of Chicago, Chicago (1993) and his MFA from the University of California, Irvine (1997). This was followed by a period as an artist-in-residence at Skowhegan School of Painting and Sculpture, Maine (1997). Newkirk's photographs, mixed media paintings and sculptural installations engage with both the personal and political realities of being identified as African American, which he often conveys through the use of disparate materials, from fake snow and white neon to the pony-beads, braided hair and pomade associated with black hairstyles. Newkirk's recent solo exhibitions include the Museum of Contemporary Art, San Diego (2005), Art Gallery of Ontario,

Toronto (2005) and the Museum of Contemporary Art, Cleveland (2004). His work has been presented in numerous group exhibitions, most recently *Collection in Context: Selections from the Permanent Collection* (2006) and *Freestyle* (2001), both at the Studio Museum, Harlem (2006), *Dak'Art*, 7th Edition of the Biennale of Contemporary African Art, Dakar (2006), the *Whitney Biennial: Day for Night*, Whitney Museum of American Art, New York (2006), *Uncertain States of America*, Astrup Fearnley Museum of Modern Art, Oslo (2005, travelling) and the *California Biennial*, Orange County Museum of Art, Newport Beach (2004). Newkirk was awarded the 2004 William H. Johnson Prize. He lives and works in Los Angeles.

YINKA SHONIBARE MBE

Yinka Shonibare MBE was born in London in 1962 and raised in Nigeria. He studied for his BA at the Byam Shaw School of Art, London (1984–89) and completed his MA at Goldsmiths College, London (1991). Known primarily for his figurative sculptures inspired by literature and art history rendered in recognisably African fabrics, Shonibare's works bring together disparate cultural references and materials, to explore issues around colonisation and exploration, national and racial identity, and class and cultural politics. His recent solo exhibitions include the Museum Boijmans Van Beuningen, Rotterdam (2004), Kunsthalle Wien, Vienna (2004), Fabric Workshop and Museum, Philadelphia (2004), KIASMA Museum of Contemporary Art, Helsinki (2003), Studio Museum, Harlem (2002) and Camden Arts Centre, London (2000). His work has been exhibited internationally in group exhibitions such as *Around the World in Eighty Days*, Institute of Contemporary Arts, London and South London Gallery (2006), *Figures in the Field: Figurative Sculpture and Abstract Painting from Chicago*, Museum of Contemporary Art, Chicago (2006), *Take Two Worlds and Views: Contemporary Art from the Collection*, Museum of Modern Art, New York (2006), *Translation*, Palais de Tokyo, Paris (2005), *Africa Remix*, Museum Kunst Palast, Düsseldorf (2004, travelling), *Documenta 11*, Kassel (2002), *The Short Century*, Museum Villa Stuck, Munich (2001, travelling), *Plateau of Mankind*, 49th International Art Exhibition, La Biennale di Venezia, Venice (2001) and *Sensation: Young British Art from the Saatchi Collection*, Royal Academy, London (1997). In 2005 Shonibare was awarded an MBE in the Queen's New Year Honours List for services to art, and in 2004 he was short-listed for the Turner Prize. He lives and works in London.

ERIC WESLEY

Eric Wesley was born in Los Angeles in 1973 and studied at the University of California, Los Angeles (1992–97). Wesley operates in the area of formal as well as social critique, his playfully subversive practice often taking the form of large-scale installations directed at contemporary global culture, whether television programmes, art institutions, food production or the weapons trade. His first solo exhibition in a public art institution was presented at the Museum of Contemporary Art, Los Angeles (2006) as part of the MOCA Focus Programme. Wesley has been included in a number of group exhibitions, including *100 Artists See God*, Institute of Contemporary Arts, London (2004–05, travelling), the *Whitney Biennial*, Whitney Museum of American Art, New York (2004), *More Boots=Many Routes*, Transmission Gallery, Glasgow (2003), *Snapshot: New Art from Los Angeles*, UCLA Hammer Museum, Los Angeles and the Museum of Contemporary Art, North Miami (2001), and *Freestyle*, Studio Museum, New York and Santa Monica Museum of Art, Santa Monica (2001). Wesley lives and works in Los Angeles and Berlin.

MARIO YBARRA JR.

Mario Ybarra Jr. was born in Los Angeles in 1973. He received his BFA from Otis College of Art and Design, Los Angeles (1999) and his MFA in Studio Art from the University of California, Irvine (2001). Ybarra's art practice – working across a range of media including drawing, installation, video and photography – engages with the social conditions of contemporary Los Angeles and his own experiences as a Mexican American artist living in the city. His work has been presented in a number of group exhibitions, including the *Tijuana Biennial*, Centro Cultural Tijuana, Tijuana (2006), *Consider This...*, LACMA Lab, Los Angeles County Museum of Art, Los Angeles (2006), *Home of the Free*, Hyde Park Art Center, Chicago (2005), and *Uncertain States of America*, Astrup Fearnley Museum of Modern Art, Oslo (2005). His performances include *Art Perform*, Art Basel Miami Beach, Miami (2005), *Below the Belt*, Los Angeles Contemporary Exhibitions, Los Angeles (2003) and *A Show That Will Show That A Show Is Not Just A Show*, The Project, Los Angeles (2002). In 2002 Ybarra co-founded Slanguage in Wilmington, California and in 2006, with his partner Karla B. Diaz, he opened a project space, also in Los Angeles, called the New Chinatown Barbershop. He lives and works in Los Angeles.

LIST OF WORKS

WORKS IN THE EXHIBITION

Laylah Ali
Untitled (Types), 2004
Mixed media on paper
27.9 x 19.1 cm
Collection Disaphol Chansiri,
Bangkok

Untitled (Types), 2004
Mixed media on paper
27.9 x 19.1 cm
Courtesy Miller Block Gallery,
Boston

Untitled (Types), 2004
Mixed media on paper
27.9 x 19.1 cm
Courtesy Miller Block Gallery,
Boston

Untitled (Types), 2004
Oil pastel and watercolour
pencil on paper
27.9 x 19.1 cm
Courtesy Miller Block Gallery,
Boston

Untitled (Types), 2004
Oil pastel and watercolour
pencil on paper
38.3 x 28.4 cm
Courtesy Miller Block Gallery,
Boston

Untitled (Types), 2004
Oil pastel and watercolour
pencil on paper
38.1 x 27.9 cm
Collection Daniel and Rena
Sternberg, Glencoe, Illinois

Hamad Butt
The Triffid (part II of the
Transmission installation), 1990
U-matic video transferred to DVD
17 minutes, 8 seconds
Courtesy Ahmad Butt, London

Ellen Gallagher
and **Edgar Cleijne**
Murmur, 2003–04
Five 16mm animation-film
projections
Blizzard of White, 55 second loop
Watery Ecstatic, 5 minute,
44 second loop
Monster, 4 minute, 51 second loop
Super Boo, 1 minute,
50 second loop
Kabuki, 1 minute, 49 second loop
Dimensions variable
© Ellen Gallagher/Edgar Cleijne
Courtesy the artists and Hauser
& Wirth Zürich London

David Huffman
It's All Over Now, Baby Blue,
2006
Mixed media on wood
203.2 x 243.8 x 2.54 cm
Courtesy the artist and Patricia
Sweetow Gallery, San Francisco

Hew Locke
Golden Horde, 2006
Mixed media (plastic, wood,
metal and fabric)
Dimensions variable
Courtesy the artist and
Hales Gallery, London

Marepe
Untitled, 2002
Christmas ornaments
53 x 20 x 32 cm
Collection Laura Skoler,
New York

Untitled, 2002
Christmas ornaments
65 x 60 x 44 cm
Collection Steven D. Corkin,
Boston

Untitled, 2002
Christmas ornaments
70 x 50 x 26 cm
Courtesy Galeria Fortes Vilaça,
São Paulo

Untitled, 2002
Christmas ornaments
29 x 50 x 30 cm
Courtesy Galeria Luisa Strina,
São Paulo

Untitled, 2002
Christmas ornaments
38 x 30 x 30 cm
Courtesy Galerie Nathalie
Obadia, Paris

Untitled, 2002
Christmas ornaments
54 x 30.5 x 40 cm
Private Collection, New York
Courtesy Anton Kern Gallery,
New York

Untitled, 2002
Christmas ornaments
35.6 x 27.9 x 25.4 cm
Courtesy the artist, Anton Kern
Gallery, New York and Galeria
Luisa Strina, São Paulo

Untitled, 2002
Christmas ornaments
53 x 20 x 32 cm
Private Collection, London

Untitled, 2002
Christmas ornaments
45 x 53 x 27 cm
Private Collection, São Paulo

Untitled, 2002
Christmas ornaments
90 x 34 x 110 cm
Private Collection, São Paulo

Untitled, 2003
Christmas ornaments
70 x 52 x 59 cm
Courtesy Galerie Nathalie
Obadia, Paris

Untitled, 2003
Christmas ornaments
60 x 35 x 35 cm
Collection Ivan Arcuschin,
São Paulo

Untitled, 2003
Christmas ornaments
30 x 57 x 34 cm
Courtesy Galeria Fortes Vilaça,
São Paulo

Untitled, 2003
Christmas ornaments
40 x 47 x 34 cm
Courtesy Galeria Luisa Strina,
São Paulo

Untitled, 2003
Christmas ornaments
31 x 65 x 43 cm
Courtesy Galeria Luisa Strina,
São Paulo

Untitled, 2003
Christmas ornaments
15 x 39 x 35 cm
Courtesy Galeria Luisa Strina,
São Paulo

Untitled, 2003
Christmas ornaments
90 x 90 x 65 cm
Courtesy Galeria Luisa Strina,
São Paulo

Untitled, 2003
Christmas ornaments
22 x 40 x 20 cm
Private Collection, Italy

Untitled, 2004
Christmas ornaments
22.9 x 67 x 34.9 cm
Courtesy the artist, Anton Kern
Gallery, New York and Galeria
Luisa Strina, São Paulo

Untitled, 2004
Christmas ornaments
18.1 x 39.1 x 40 cm
Courtesy the artist, Anton Kern
Gallery, New York and Galeria
Luisa Strina, São Paulo

Untitled, 2004
Christmas ornaments
10.6 x 9.5 x 17.4 cm
Private Collection, Italy

Henna Nadeem
Bridge and Bay, 2006
Digital montage
Image size 31.5 x 36 cm
Commissioned by Photoworks
Courtesy the artist and
Photoworks

Lone Tree, 2006
Digital montage
Image size 31.5 x 36 cm
Commissioned by Photoworks
Courtesy the artist and
Photoworks

Modern Building, 2006
Digital montage
Image size 31.5 x 36 cm
Commissioned by Photoworks
Courtesy the artist and
Photoworks

Orange/Tree, 2006
Digital montage
Image size 31.5 x 36 cm
Commissioned by Photoworks
Courtesy the artist and
Photoworks

People, 2006
Digital montage
Image size 31.5 x 36 cm
Commissioned by Photoworks
Courtesy the artist and
Photoworks

Plan, 2006
Digital montage
Image size 31.5 x 36 cm
Commissioned by Photoworks
Courtesy the artist and
Photoworks

Street, 2006
Digital montage
Image size 31.5 x 36 cm
Commissioned by Photoworks
Courtesy the artist and
Photoworks

Streetstar, 2006
Digital montage
Image size 31.5 x 36 cm
Commissioned by Photoworks
Courtesy the artist and
Photoworks

Trees, 2006
Digital montage
Image size 31.5 x 36 cm
Commissioned by Photoworks
Courtesy the artist and
Photoworks

Winter, 2006
Digital montage
Image size 31.5 x 36 cm
Commissioned by Photoworks
Courtesy the artist and
Photoworks

Kori Newkirk
Merk, 2006
Pony beads, artificial hair
extensions, aluminium and dye
Approx. 238.7 x 183 x 2.5 cm
Courtesy the artist and
The Project, New York

Yinka Shonibare MBE
Dysfunctional Family, 1999
Wax-printed cotton, polyester,
wood and plastic
Four sculptures in total
Father: 148 x 52.1 x 38.1 cm
Boy: 88.9 x 54 x 45.8 cm
Mother: 149.9 x 40 x 35.6 cm
Girl: 68.6 x 35.6 x 30.5 cm
Collection Walker Art Center,
Minneapolis. Butler Family
Fund, 2000

Eric Wesley
Home base one, 2006
Folding table and mixed media
Dimensions variable
Courtesy the artist

Home base two, 2006
Folding table and mixed media
Dimensions variable
Courtesy the artist

Terminal, 2006
Wall mounted and freestanding
reflective mirrors
Wall mounted: approx. 15.2 x
15.2 x 15.2 cm; freestanding:
15.2 x 15.2 x 121.9 cm
Courtesy the artist

Untitled, 2006
Remote controlled mylar
saucer/blimp
Approx. 96.5 x 96.5 x 121.9 cm
Courtesy the artist

Mario Ybarra Jr.
Brown and Proud, 2006
Mixed media
Dimensions variable
Courtesy the artist

ORIGINAL FILM POSTERS
IN THE EXHIBITION

Artist unknown
The Day the Earth Stood Still,
1951
Original US, linen backed
104.1 x 68.6 cm
Courtesy of the Damian
Harland Collection, London

Artist unknown
The Thing from Another World,
1951
Original US, paper backed
48.3 x 35.6 cm
Courtesy of The Reel Poster
Gallery, London

Artist unknown
*The Quatermass Experiment /
Zemsta Kosmosu*, 1955
Original Polish, linen backed
83.8 x 58.4 cm
Courtesy of the Hastings
Collections, Los Angeles

Artist unknown
Forbidden Planet, 1956
Original US
104.1 x 68.6 cm
Courtesy of the Peter Douglass
Collection, London

Artist unknown
Invasion of the Body Snatchers,
1956
Original US, linen backed
104.1 x 68.6 cm
Courtesy of The Reel Poster
Gallery, London

Reynold Brown
This Island, Earth, 1955
Original US, paper backed
57.8 x 71.1 cm (Style B)
Courtesy of the Vincent Palser
Collection, London

Reynold Brown
The Day of the Triffids, 1962
Original US, linen backed
104.1 x 68.6 cm
Courtesy of The Reel Poster
Gallery, London

Franco Fiorenzi
*The War of the Worlds /
La Guerra dei Mondi*, 1953
Original Italian, linen backed
201 x 140 cm
Courtesy of The Reel Poster
Gallery, London

Clement Hurel
*Quatermass II: Enemy from
Space / Terre contre Satellite*,
1957
Original French, linen backed
160 x 119.4 cm
Courtesy of The Reel Poster
Gallery, London

Joseph Smith
It Came from Outer Space, 1953
Original US, linen backed
205.7 x 104.1 cm
Courtesy of the Andy Johnson
Collection, London

LIST OF ILLUSTRATIONS

PP 46–47
David Huffman
Get Up and Get Down, 2006
Mixed media on paper
127 x 247 cm
Courtesy the artist and Patricia
Sweetow Gallery, San Francisco

PP 48–49
Hew Locke
Golden Horde, 2006 (details)
Mixed media (plastic, wood,
metal and fabric)
Dimensions variable
Courtesy the artist and Hales
Gallery, London
Photograph: Roberto Rubalcava

P. 50, TOP LEFT
Marepe
Untitled, 2002
Christmas ornaments
53 x 20 x 32 cm
Private Collection, London

TOP RIGHT
Marepe
Untitled, 2002
Christmas ornaments
65 x 60 x 44 cm
Collection Steven D. Corkin,
Boston

BOTTOM LEFT
Marepe
Untitled, 2002
Christmas ornaments
29 x 50 x 30 cm
Courtesy Galeria Luisa Strina,
São Paulo

BOTTOM RIGHT
Marepe
Untitled, 2002
Christmas ornaments
70 x 50 x 26 cm
Courtesy Galeria Fortes Vilaça,
São Paulo

P. 53
Henna Nadeem
Plan, 2006
Digital montage
Image size 31.5 x 36 cm
Commissioned by Photoworks
Courtesy the artist
and Photoworks

PP 54–55
Kori Newkirk
Drawing for *Merk*, 2006
Computer-generated drawing
Courtesy the artist and
The Project, New York

P. 57
Yinka Shonibare MBE
Dysfunctional Family, 1999

Wax-printed cotton, polyester,
wood and plastic
Four sculptures in total
Father: 148 x 52.1 x 38.1 cm
Boy: 88.9 x 54 x 45.8 cm
Mother: 149.9 x 40 x 35.6 cm
Girl: 68.6 x 35.6 x 30.5 cm
Collection Walker Art Center,
Minneapolis. Butler Family
Fund, 2000

P. 58
Eric Wesley
Plan for *Untitled*, 2006
Computer-generated drawing
Courtesy the artist

PP 60–61
Mario Ybarra Jr.
Sketch for *Brown and Proud*, 2006
Graphite on paper
Courtesy the artist

PP 62–63
Ellen Gallagher and
Edgar Cleijne
Monster (Murmur), 2003–04
16mm film stills
© Ellen Gallagher/Edgar
Cleijne, Courtesy the artists
and Hauser & Wirth
Zürich London

P. 68
Set photograph from *The
Quatermass Experiment* (BBC
Productions, TV series, UK),
1953, Dir. Nigel Kneale
Image courtesy of BBC

P. 71
Set photograph from
Quatermass and the Pit (BBC
Productions, TV series, UK),
1958–59, Dir. Nigel Kneale
Image courtesy of BBC

P. 72
Set photograph from
Quatermass and the Pit (BBC
Productions, TV series, UK),
1958–59, Dir. Nigel Kneale
Image courtesy of BBC

P. 73, LEFT
Sir Jacob Epstein
*Torso in Metal from
'The Rock Drill'*, 1913–14
Bronze
© Tate, London 2006

RIGHT
Bryan Kneale
Crayfish, 1955
Oil on canvas
Courtesy of Judith Kerr and
Nigel Kneale
Photograph: Roberto Rubalcava

PP 74–75
Eagle magazine, 4 July 1952
Image courtesy of
The Culture Archive
Reproduced by kind permission
of the Dan Dare Corporation

P. 76
Set photograph from *The
Quatermass Experiment* (BBC
Productions, TV series, UK),
1953, Dir. Nigel Kneale
Image courtesy of BBC

PP 78–79
Set photograph from
Quatermass and the Pit (BBC
Productions, TV series, UK),
1958–59, Dir. Nigel Kneale
Image courtesy of BBC

P. 81
Set photograph from
Quatermass and the Pit (BBC
Productions, TV series, UK),
1958–59, Dir. Nigel Kneale
Image courtesy of BBC

P. 82
Photograph of Louis Leakey
Used with permission from
The Leakey Foundation

P. 83
Original clipping from
The Illustrated London News,
17 January 1953
Used with permission from
The Illustrated London News

P. 85
Page from *The Illustrated
London News*, 13 September 1958
Used with permission from
The Illustrated London News

P. 90
Artist unknown
The Thing from Another World,
1951
Original US film poster,
paper backed
48.3 x 35.6 cm
Courtesy of The Reel Poster
Gallery, London

P. 91
Clement Hurel
*Quatermass II: Enemy from
Space/Terre contre Satellite*,
1957
Original French film poster,
linen backed
160 x 119.4 cm
Courtesy of The Reel Poster
Gallery, London

P. 92
Joseph Smith
It Came from Outer Space, 1953
Original US film poster,
linen backed
205.7 x 104.1 cm
Courtesy of the Andy Johnson
Collection, London

P. 93
Artist unknown
*The Quatermass Experiment/
Zemsta Kosmosu*, 1955
Original Polish film poster,
linen backed
83.8 x 58.4 cm
Courtesy of the Hastings
Collections, Los Angeles

P. 94
Artist unknown
Forbidden Planet, 1956
Original US film poster,
104.1 x 68.6 cm
Courtesy of the Peter Douglass
Collection, London

P. 98
Reynold Brown
This Island, Earth, 1955
Original US film poster,
paper backed
57.8 x 71.1 cm (Style B)
Courtesy of the Vincent Palser
Collection, London

P. 99
Franco Fiorenzi
*The War of the Worlds/
La Guerra dei Mondi*, 1953
Original Italian film poster,
linen backed
201 x 140 cm
Courtesy of The Reel Poster
Gallery, London

P. 102
Artist unknown
Children of the Damned, 1964
Original US film poster,
104.1 x 68.6 cm
Courtesy of The Reel Poster
Gallery, London

P.107
Artist unknown
This Island Earth, 1955
Original US film poster,
152.4 x 101.6 cm (Style B)
Courtesy of The Reel Poster
Archive, London

GLOSSARY OF EXTRA-TERRESTRIAL BEINGS

A

Abe Abe's Oddysee

Abh Crest of the Stars

Abyormenites Hal Clement's *Cycle of Fire* floating balloons – one race, that is

Acquarans Farscape

Advents Guyver rumored to be groups of different aliens, also known as Uranus or the Creators

Aeodronians Battlelords of the 23rd Century

Affront Iain M. Banks' Excession

Amaut C. J. Cherryh's Alliance-Union universe

Amnioni Stephen Donaldson's The Gap Cycle

Amorphs Schlock Mercenary

Anabis The Voyage of the Space Beagle by A. E. van Vogt

Ancients Farscape

Ancients Stargate SG-1

Andalites K. A. Applegate's Animorphs

Andorians Star Trek

Andromeni Battlelords of the 23rd Century

Angosians Star Trek

Androsynth Star Control

Angol Mois Sgt. Frog

Annihilus native of the Negative *Zone* Marvel Comics

The Anti-Monitor DC Comics

Antedeans Star Trek

Arachnids Battlelords of the 23rd Century

Aras Perry Rhodan

Arcturians Star Trek

Arilou Star Control

Argolin Doctor Who

Arkonides Perry Rhodan

The Arisians and Eddorians E. E. Smith's Lensman novels

Aschen Stargate SG-1

Asgard Stargate SG-1

Atevi C. J. Cherryh's Foreigner series

Aurelians Advent Rising

Auronar Blake's 7

Autobot Transformers

Autons Doctor Who

Azgonians Perry Rhodan

Aziam Battlelords of the 23rd Century

Azurite Iffix Y Santaph's StarFrost See links at Chizora

B

Baalols Perry Rhodan

Babel fish Douglas Adams's Hitchhiker's Guide series

Badoon Marvel Comics

Bailies machine race that conquered Earth in Cleopatra 2525

Bajorans Star Trek

Ba'kus Star Trek

Balmarians Super Robot Wars

Bandersnatchi Slaver's meat animal in Larry Niven's Known Space

Bandi Star Trek

Banik Farscape

Barkonides Perry Rhodan

Banthas Star Wars

Beings of the Extra Terrestrial origin which is Adversary of human race Muv-Luv

Benjari Battlelords of the 23rd Century

Benzites Star Trek

Berserkers of Fred Saberhagen's Berserker series

Betazoid Star Trek

Bgztlans DC Comics' Legion of Super-Heroes

Bjorn Space Quest

Black Cloud Fred Hoyle interstellar dust cloud

Blastaar native of the Negative Zone Marvel Comics

Bolians Star Trek

Boolite Farscape

Borg Star Trek

Bothans Star Wars

Braalians DC Comics' Legion of Super-Heroes

Bradicor Schlock Mercenary

Brains Win, Lose and Kaboom

Breen Star Trek

Brood Marvel Comics

Brunnen G Lexx

Budong Farscape

Bugs from Klendathu Starship Troopers

Buggers See Formics

Bynars Star Trek

Black Arms Shadow The Hedgehog video game

C

Caleban Frank Herbert's *Whipping Star* invisible telepathic beings who are actually the minds of stars

Caliban C. J. Cherryh's Alliance-Union universe

Cardassians Star Trek

Carggites DC Comics' Legion of Super-Heroes

Cat People Marvel Comics

Catalytes Utopia

Catteni Anne McCaffrey's Catteni Series

Celestials Marvel Comics

Centauri Babylon 5

Ceti eels Star Trek II: The Wrath of Khan bug-like ear parasites from Ceti Alpha V

Centrans Christopher Anvil's Pandora's Planet stories

Chalnoths Star Trek

Changelings Star Trek

Chaos Independence War aka I-War, and Independence War 2: Edge of Chaos

Charrids Farscape

Chatilians Battlelords of the 23rd Century

Chelonians Doctor Who novels

Chenjesu Star Control

Chevanno Utopia

Chi C. J. Cherryh's Chanur novels

Chigs Space: Above and Beyond

Chizora Iffix Santaph's StarFrost

Chmmr Star Control

Cho-choi Jack McDevitt's Infinity Beach

Chozo Metroid

Cirronians Tracker

Cinnrusskin James White's Sector General series

Cizerack Battlelords of the 23rd Century

Clutch Turtles Liaden universe

Coeurl The Voyage of the Space Beagle by A. E. van Vogt

Colatas Farscape

Cole "Tracker"

Colour out of space H. P. Lovecraft

Coluans DC Comics'

Legion of Super-Heroes

Combine an alien empire in Half-Life 2, note: many of the "Combine" seen in the game are actually humans that have been assimilated or collaborate as brutal police troopers

Coneheads Native inhabitants of the planet Remulak they are recognized by their distinctive craniums which are roughly conical in shape.

Coreeshi Farscape

Corporal Giroro Sgt. Frog

The Covenant collection of religiously-motivated allied species in the Xbox/PC game Halo: Combat Evolved

Crites carnivorous hairballs of the Critters films

Cryons Doctor Who

Ctarl-Ctarl Outlaw Star

Cybermen Doctor Who

Cybertrons The Transformers

Cybyota Orion's Arm

Cylons Battlestar Galactica

D

Daemonites Wildstorm

Dakkamites Marvel Comics

Daleks Doctor Who

The Dance Marvel Comics

Darjakr'Ul Utopia

Dark Eldar Warhammer 40,000

Darrians Traveller RPG known for their small, high-technology polity

Daxamites DC Comics

Decepticon Transformers

Deep Ones H. P. Lovecraft

Delvians Farscape

Deneans Farscape

Denebians Star Trek

Denobulans Star Trek

Dentics Farscape

Dentrassis "Hitchhikers Guide to the Galaxy"

Deltans Star Trek

Dessarians Tracker

Diamondhead Ben 10

Dilbians Ursinoid species of The Law-Twister Shorty and other stories by Gordon Dickson

Dnyarri Star Control

Dominators DC Comics

Dominators Doctor Who

the Doublers two-in-one semi-humanoids of Stanisław Lem's Eden

Dracs Barry B. Longyear's Enemy Mine and The Enemy Papers

Draconians Doctor Who

Drahvins Doctor Who

Draic Kin The Longest Journey, Dreamfall

Draaknaars Thor series

Drak Farscape

Drakh Babylon 5 & Crusade

Druuge Star Control

Duos from Uranus Space Patrol 1962 TV series

Durlans DC Comics' Legion of Super-Heroes

Dugs Star Wars

Dyson Aliens Peter F. Hamilton's "Pandora's Star"

E

Edo Star Trek

Ego the Living Planet Marvel Comics

Ekhonides Perry Rhodan

Eldar Warhammer 40,000

El-Aurians Star Trek

Elder Gods Cthulhu Mythos

Elder Things Cthulhu Mythos

Eldorians Utopia

Elitians

Energy Rider Farscape

Ep-Hogers Perry Rhodan

Eridani Battlelords of the 23rd Century

Esmers Little Big Adventure 2, they are divided into four races: *Sups, Francos, Wannies and Mosquibees*

E.T Extra Terrestrial being in the movie "E.T. The Extra-Terrestrial"

Ewoks Star Wars

F

The Face of Boe Doctor Who

The Fendahl Doctor Who

Ferengi Wheeling and dealing humanoids from Star Trek

Ferronans Perry Rhodan

Festival Singularity Sky by Charles Stross

Flatcats Robert A. Heinlein's novel The Rolling Stones, compare Tribble

Foamasi Doctor Who

Foralbo Utopia

The Forest of Cheem Doctor Who

Formics Ender Wiggins cycle by Orson Scott Card.

Fott Battlelords of the 23rd Century

F'sherl-Ganni Schlock Mercenary, also called 'Gatekeepers'

Furbls Battlelords of the 23rd Century

Furlings Stargate SG1 — member of the Four Great Races

Furons Destroy All Humans!

Fithp "Baby Elephants" from Larry Niven's Footfall

G

Gaim Babylon 5

Galactus Planet-devouring force of nature in Marvel Comics

Galaxoid Calvin and Hobbes by Bill Watterson

Garthlings David Brin's Uplift Universe

The Gelth Doctor Who

Gemini Battlelords of the 23rd Century

Gethenians Ursula Le Guins Ekumen stories and other races

Ghamans Perry Rhodan

Gigan from the Godzilla films

G'keks David Brin's Uplift Universe

Gladifers Dennis Paul Himes

Gloarft Megas XLR

Goa'uld Stargate SG-1

Gonzo The Muppets

Goola-Goola Battlelords of the 23rd Century

Gorlocks Win, Lose and Kaboom

Gorn Star Trek

Goszuls Perry Rhodan

Gowachin Frank Herbert's stories

Grans Star Wars

The Graske Doctor Who

Great Race of Yith H. P. Lovecraft

Grogs Larry Niven's Known Space

Grudeks Farscape

G.R.A.I.S.E. Melonpool

Greys popular mythology

Grunds Marvel Comics

Guardians of the Universe natives of the planet Oa, creators and administrators of the Green Lantern Corps in DC Comics

Gubru David Brin's Uplift Universe

Gungans Star Wars

Gnosis Xenosaga

H

Halflings Dances in the Snow, Genome

Hallessi Harry Turtledove's Worldwar book series, a subject species of the Race

Halosians Farscape

Hangi Farscape

Hani C. J. Cherryh's Chanur novels

Headies Noon Universe

Heechee Frederik Pohl

Hirogen Star Trek

Hisa C. J. Cherryh's Alliance-Union universe

Hivers Traveller RPG modified starfish

Hooloovoo Hitchhiker's Guide series by Douglas Adams

Hoon David Brin's Uplift Universe

Horda Doctor Who

Hork-Bajir K. A. Applegate's Animorphs

Horta Star Trek

Howard the Duck Marvel Comics

Hur'q Star Trek

Hutts Star Wars

Hupyrian Star Trek

Husnock Star Trek

Hydrans Star Trek

Hykraius DC Comics' Legion of Super-Heroes

Hynerians Farscape

I

Ibs Robert J. Sawyer's Starplex

Ice Warriors Doctor Who

Iconians Star Trek

Iduve C. J. Cherryh's Alliance-Union universe

Ikrini Battlelords of the 23rd Century

Ilanics Farscape

Ilwrath Star Control

Imskians DC Comics' Legion of Super-Heroes

Interions Farscape

Invid/Inbit Flower of Life hunting conquerors of Earth from Robotech: The New Generation and their counterparts from Genesis Climber Mospeada

Ha May Bourg Eyer

Irkens Invader Zim

Isanians Perry Rhodan

Ishtarians Poul Anderson's Fire Time

Ixtl The Voyage of the Space Beagle by A. E. van Vogt

J

Jaffa Stargate SG-1

Jaridians Earth: Final Conflict

Jem'Hadar Star Trek

Jenova Final Fantasy 7

Jezzedaic Priests Battlelords of the 23rd Century

J'naii Star Trek

Jocaceans Farscape

Jotoki Larry Niven's Known Space

K

Kafers 2300AD

Kaleds Doctor Who

Kalish Farscape

Kal-Kriken Utopia

Kalliran C. J. Cherryh's Alliance-Union universe

Karrema Star Trek

Kazon Star Trek

Kdatlyno Larry Niven's Known Space

Kerons Sgt. Frog

Key-Guardians Utopia

Kherubim Wildstorm

Khunds DC Comics

Khurtarnan Farscape

Kif C. J. Cherryh's Chanur novels

Kilaaks Destroy All Monsters

Kilrathi Wing Commander games

Kizanti Battlelords of the 23rd Century

Klingons Star Trek

Knnn C. J. Cherryh's Chanur novels

Koozbanians The Muppet Show

Korbinites Marvel Comics

K-PAXians K-PAX

Krakeds Battlelords of the 23rd Century

Kren See Chizora

Kree Marvel Comics

Kreely Schlock Mercenary

Krith Richard C Merediths 'Timeliner Trilogy'

Kromaggs Sliders

Kroot Warhammer 40,000

Krynoids Doctor Who

Kryptonians DC Comics

Kssthrata Schlock Mercenary

Kymnar FTL:2448 RPG

Kymellians Horse head w/ humanoid body; Marvel Comics

Kyo C. J. Cherryh's Foreigner series

Kyulek O.R.B: Off-World Resource Base

Kzinti Larry Niven's Known Space series and Star Trek: The Animated Series

L

Lallorans DC Comics' Legion of Super-Heroes

Lance Corporal Dororo Sgt. Frog

Laxidasians Marvel Comics

Lectroids The Adventures of Buckaroo Banzai Across the Eighth Dimension

Leerans Animorphs by K. A. Applegate

Leviathan Farscape

Lithians James Blish's A Case of Conscience

Livrai Hostile aliens encountered in Joe Haldeman's Mindbridge

Lombaxes Ratchet & Clank

Loomi Space Patrol creatures inhabiting Jupiter with heat-retaining skins.

Lucratians Utopia

Lunarians Final Fantasy IV

Lurmans Doctor Who

Luxans Farscape

Ly-Cilph The Night's Dawn Trilogy

Lyrans Star Fleet Universe

M

M-113 Star Trek

Macra Doctor Who

Mahendo'sat C. J. Cherryh's Chanur novels
Maians Perfect Dark
Magog Andromeda
Majat C. J. Cherryh's Alliance-Union universe
Marklars South Park
Martians H. G. Wells' The War of the Worlds
Edgar Rice Burroughs's Barsoom series
Ray Bradbury's The Martian Chronicles
Aelita 1924 movie
Mars Attacks! Topps trading cards and Tim Burton movie
Quatermass and the Pit BBC science-fiction television serial
Larry Niven's Known Space... and many others
Masters The Tripods
Mazians Battlelords of the 23rd Century
Meehooks the comic book series Fusion, "dinosaurs with fur"
Melmacians ALF
Melnorme Star Control
Melotians Melonpool
Menoptra Doctor Who
Mentors Doctor Who
Merseians Technic History by Poul Anderson
Mesklinites Hal Clement's Mission of Gravity millipede-like
Methorians Barrington J. Bayley's Zen Gun gaseous giant-giant dwellers
Metroid Metroid series
Microman
Minbari Babylon 5
Mon Calamari Star Wars
Minosians Star Trek
Mintakans Star Trek
Miradorn Star Trek
Misha Battlelords of the 23rd Century
Mmrnmhrm Star Control
Mondoshawan The Fifth Element
The Mooninites individually: Igninokt and Err Aqua Teen Hunger Force
Monoids Doctor Who
Mork "Mork and Mindy"
Morlocks H. G. Wells' The Time Machine
Larry Niven's Known Space
Moroks Doctor Who
Mor-Taxans the aliens from the first season of War of the Worlds
Morthren the aliens in the second season of War of the Worlds
Movellans Doctor Who
Moxx of Balhoon Doctor Who
Mri C. J. Cherryh's Faded Sun trilogy
Mudokons Oddworld series
Mutzachans Battlelords of the

23rd Century
Muuh from Orion's Arm
Mycon Star Control

N
Naglon Doctor Who
Nairnama Independence War, aka I-War
Narn Babylon 5
Namekian Dragon Ball
Nausicaans Star Trek
Neadlehead Win, Lose and Kaboom
Nebari Farscape
Nebular Calvin and Hobbes by Bill Waterson
Necrons Warhammer 40,000
Nemet C. J. Cherryh's Alliance-Union universe
Neutrals Futurama
New Gods From the planets Apokolips and New Genesis, from The Fourth World in DC Comics
Niea Niea 7
Nietzscheans Andromeda
Nihilanth Half-Life
Nodulians Tracker
Nox Stargate SG-1
Nomes Terry Pratchett's The Bromeliad
N'Kull Advent Rising
Nyronds passim in the works of Zander Nyrond; occasionally in those of his "brother" Soren

O
Oankali Octavia Butler's Xenogenesis series
Ob'enn Schlock Mercenary
Ocampa Star Trek
Ogri Doctor Who
Ogrons Doctor Who
Omicronians / Popplers Futurama
Optera Doctor Who
Orandoans DC Comics' Legion of Super-Heroes
Orsians Tracker
Orion Rogues Battlelords of the 23rd Century
Orks Warhammer 40,000
Orkans Mork and Mindy
Ortheans Mary Gentle's Golden Witchbreed androgynous until puberty
Outsiders Larry Niven's species from Known Space
Overlords Childhood's End by Arthur C. Clarke
Orz Star Control

P
Paan'uri the Dark Matter Entities from Schlock Mercenary
Pak or Protectors Larry Niven's Known Space books The superintelligent adult form of homo habilis; human Protectors are even more intelligent.
Pakled Star Trek
Parillatians Utopia

Pascalenes Utopia
Pascians Battlelords of the 23rd Century
Peliar Zel Star Trek
Phagors Brian W. Aldiss's Heliconia series
Phalanx Marvel Comics
Phleebhutinskis Space Quest
Phtagurs Metabarons
Pierson's Puppeteers Larry Niven's Ringworld and Known Space series three legs, two manipulative heads
Pilots Farscape
Pinkunz Space Quest
Pkunk Star Control
Pequeninos Orson Scott Card's Speaker for the Dead
Posleen John Ringo's "Legacy of the Aldenata"
Phentari Battlelords of the 23rd Century
*Pr?*tans* The High Crusade
"Predator" aliens See Yautja
Primes Peter F. Hamilton's "Commonwealth Saga"
Private Tamama Sgt. Frog
Progenitors David Brin's Uplift Universe
Prophets Star Trek
Protoss StarCraft
Psychlos Battlefield Earth
Psychons Space: 1999
Prot Gene Brewer's K-PAX
Protoculture Macross series advanced race who engineered humans and Zentradi
The Puppet Masters
Purple Aliens It's Walky!; according to their leader, 'Alien' is the name of their homeworld in their own language
Python Lizards Battlelords of the 23rd Century

Q
Q Star Trek
Quarks Doctor Who
Quarren "Squid Heads" Star Wars
Quintesson Transformers
Qwardians DC Comics

R
Rabotevs Harry Turtledove's Worldwar book series, a subject species of the Race
Race The Moreau Series Amoeboid aliens that attempt to hide on an Earth where genetic engineering has been rampant
The Race Harry Turtledove's Worldwar book series, a reptillian species that had conquered two planets and attacked "Tosev 3" Earth in 1942
Rako-Gorda Utopia
Ram Pythons Battlelords of the 23rd Century
Re'tu Stargate SG-1

Reapers Doctor Who
Regul C. J. Cherryh's Alliance-Union universe
Relgarians Farscape
Remans Star Trek
Replicators Stargate SG-1
Rigellians Simpsons The Simpsons including Kang and Kodos
Rigellians Lensman books which are barrel-shaped with four tentacular arms and four stubby legs
Riim The Voyage of the Space Beagle by A. E. van Vogt
Rills Doctor Who
Risan Star Trek
Rodians Star Wars
Romulans Star Trek
Rull The War against the Rull by A. E. van Vogt
Rutans Doctor Who

S
Sal-Kadeem Utopia
Sandworm Dune
Saiyan Dragon Ball
Sarturians Utopia
Mr. Saturn EarthBound
Sau-Bau Battlelords of the 23rd Century
Scarrens Farscape
Scorvians Farscape
Scrin Command & Conquer
Sebaceans Farscape
Second through Last Men Olaf Stapledon's Last and First Men
Sergeant Keroro Sgt. Frog
Sergeant Major Kururu Sgt. Frog
Sariens Space Quest
Shadows Babylon 5
Sharrh C. J. Cherryh's Alliance-Union universe
Sheeda Grant Morrison's Seven soldiers of Victory megaseries
Sheliak Star Trek
Sheyangs Farscape
Shi'ar Marvel Comics
Shingouz Valérian comics
Shivans Descent: FreeSpace
Shoggoths H. P. Lovecraft
Shofixti Star Control
Shonunin C. J. Cherryh's Alliance-Union universe
Shroobs Mario & Luigi: Partners in Time
Silver Surfer Marvel Comics
Skaarj Unreal Tournament
Skedar Perfect Dark
Skrulls Marvel Comics
Slavers see also Thrint
Slitheen Doctor Who
Slylandro Star Control
Snarks Marvel Comics
Solaris by Stanisław Lem living planet
Solomon Family 3rd Rock from the Sun
Son'a Star Trek
Soomanii Utopia

Soro David Brin's Uplift Universe
Sontarans Doctor Who
Space Pirates Metroid series
Spathi Star Control
Species 8472 Star Trek
Spock Star Trek
Squiz-Quijy Utopia
Strogg Quake II and Quake 4
Stsho C. J. Cherryh's Chanur novels
Suliban Star Trek
Superman Superman I-IV & Superman Returns
Supox Star Control
Sycorax Doctor Who
Sye-Men Battlelords of the 23rd Century
Sykarians Farscape
Syreen Star Control

T

T'Lani Star Trek
Taelons Gene Roddenberry's Earth: Final Conflict
Tai Genome
Talarians Star Trek
Talaxians Star Trek
Talokians DC Comics' Legion of Super-Heroes
Talosians Star Trek
Tamarians Star Trek
Tanndai Techknights Battlelords of the 23rd Century
Tandarans Star Trek
Tandu David Brin's Uplift Universe
Tarellians Star Trek
Tarkans Farscape
Tau Warhammer 40,000
Tavleks Farscape
Taxxons Animorphs series
Tc'a C. J. Cherryh's Chanur novels
Technarchy Marvel Comics
Tecreseans Battlelords of the 23rd Century
Tenctonese Alien Nation
Tenebrians Hal Clement's Close to Critical
Tellarites Star Trek
Temarkians Utopia
Terellian Star Trek
Terileptils Doctor Who
Terra Novans Star Trek
Terran Final Fantasy IX
Terrelian Star Trek
Terrellian Star Trek
Terrians Earth 2
Tetraps Doctor Who
Thals Doctor Who
Thanagarians DC Comics
Thargoids Elite game
Therons Dan Dare stories
Tholians Star Trek
Thraddash Star Control
Thranx Alan Dean Foster's Humanx Commonwealth series
Thrint Larry Niven's Known Space

Tiberians Buzz Aldrin and John Barnes' Encounter With Tiber
Tilikanthua Utopia
Time Lords of Gallifrey Doctor Who
Titanians DC Comics' Legion of Super-Heroes
Titanides John Varley's Gaea-trilogy
the Tleilaxu Frank Herbert's Dune novels
Tnuctip Species that engineered the revolt against the Thrint in Larry Niven's Known Space
Tollan Stargate Sg-1
Trabe Star Trek
Tractators Doctor Who
Traeki David Brin's Uplift Universe
Tralfamadorians Kurt Vonnegut The Sirens of Titan, Slaughterhouse 5
Tran Alan Dean Foster's Icerigger
Trandoshans Star Wars
Traskans Farscape
Treecats David Weber' 'Honorverse'
Treens Dan Dare stories
Tribbles Star Trek; compare the earlier flatcats from Robert A. Heinlein's The Rolling Stones
Triceraton Teenage Mutant Ninja Turtles
Trills Star Trek
Trillions Nicholas Fisk small collective crystals
Trinocs Larry Niven's Known Space
Tromites DC Comics' Legion of Super-Heroes
Tsufurujin Dragon Ball
Tusken Raiders Star Wars
Twi'leks Star Wars
Twinsunians Little Big Adventure, they are divided into four races: Quetches, Rabbibunnies, Grobos and Spheros
Tyranids Warhammer 40,000

U

U'tani Star Trek
Unas Stargate SG-1
The Uncreated Marvel Comics
Umgah Star Control
Uniocs Schlock Mercenary
Unity Superman: The Animated Series
Ur-Quan Kzer-Za Star Control
Ur-Quan Kohr-Ah Star Control
Uryuoms El Goonish Shive
Utrom Teenage Mutant Ninja Turtles
Utwig Star Control

V

Vaadwaur Star Trek
Vademon Digimon
Vanacancia Utopia
Varga plants Doctor Who

Vardians Tracker
Vasudans Descent: FreeSpace
Velantians Lensman books notable for their multiplicity of eyes and various appendages
Venek Farscape
Venom and Carnage Marvel Comics
Venom grubs Doctor Who
Vervoids Doctor Who
Vhorwed Schlock Mercenary
Vidiians Star Trek
Vilani Traveller RPG known for their bureaucratic tendencies and empire building
Vilgax Ben 10
Viltrumites Invincible
Vineans Yoko Tsuno blue skin comic
Visitors V
Vogons bad poetry and bureaucratic planetary demolitions a speciality, from Douglas Adams's Hitchhiker's Guide series
Vorc Farscape
Vorcarian bloodtracker Farscape
Vorlons Babylon 5
Vorta Star Trek
Vortex life forms Ecco the Dolphin
Vorticon Commander Keen
Vortigaunt Half-Life
Vortisaurs Doctor Who audio dramas
Voth Star Trek
Vroarscans Utopia
Vulcans Star Trek
VUX Star Control

W

Waldahudin Robert J. Sawyer's Starplex
Wanderers Noon Universe
The Watcher Marvel Comics
Whrloo Larry Niven's Known Space
Willis the Bouncer Red Planet
Winathians DC Comics' Legion of Super-Heroes
Wirrn Doctor Who
Wolfweeds Doctor Who
Wogneer Star Trek
Wookiees Star Wars
The Wraith Stargate Atlantis

X

X Parasites Metroid Fusion
Xandarians Marvel Comics
Xanthuans DC Comics' Legion of Super-Heroes
Xarians Battlelords of the 23rd Century
Xel'Naga StarCraft
Xenomorphs the Alien movies
Xilians from Invasion of Astro-Monster and Godzilla: Final Wars
Xindi Star Trek
X-Nauts Paper Mario: The Thousand Year Door
Xyrillian Star Trek

Y

Yag-Kosha Robert E. Howard's Tower of the Elephant humanoid elephant
Yautja Predator
Yeerks Animorphs parasitic
Yehat Star Control
Yeti Doctor Who
Yilane West of Eden series of Harry Harrison
Yip-Yips Sesame Street
Yolkians Jimmy Neutron
Yomingans Schlock Mercenary
Yridian Star Trek
Yugopotamians The Fairly Oddparents
Yuki Nagato The Melancholy of Haruhi Suzumiya
Yuuzhan Vong Star Wars

Z

Zabrak Star Wars
Zaldans Star Trek
Zalkonians Star Trek
Zarbi Doctor Who
Zenetan Farscape
Zenn-Lavians Marvel Comics
Zentradi Macross adapted as the Zentraedi in Robotech
Zen Rigeln Battlelords of the 23rd Century
Zen-Whoberis Marvel Comics
Zerg StarCraft
Zhodani Traveller RPG - renowned psychics
Zinoboppians Melonpool
Zim Invader Zim
Zoq-Fot-Pik Star Control
Zorgons are green skinned man-eating spacefaring reptilians in Zathura and warlike red skinned humanoids in the many Characters of Sluggy Freelance
Zygons Doctor Who

List of extra-terrestrials, *Wikipedia, The Free Encyclopedia.*

Date of last revision:
29 August 2006, 22:45 UTC.

Date retrieved:
5 September 2006, 15.08 UTC.
http://en.wikipedia.org/w/index.php?title=List_of_extraterrestrials_in_fiction&oldid=72703287

Primary contributors:
View the list (subject to extremely long replication lag)
Page Version ID: 72703287

ALIEN NATION
Institute of Contemporary Arts (ICA), London
17 November 2006 – 14 January 2007

Manchester Art Gallery, Manchester
17 March – 7 May 2007

Sainsbury Centre for Visual Arts, Norwich
2 October – 9 December 2007

CURATORS
John Gill
Jens Hoffmann
Gilane Tawadros

CURATORIAL SUPPORT
Claire Fitzsimmons
Cary Rajinder Sawhney
Cylena Simonds

EXHIBITION ASSISTANCE
Gemma Sharpe, Curatorial Assistant
Jen Wu, Inspire Curatorial Fellow

GALLERY MANGER, ICA
Trevor Hall

PRESS AND MARKETING, ICA
Anna Hyde, Marketing Director
Natasha Plowright, Senior Press Officer
Victoria Benjamin, Marketing Executive

PRESS AND MARKETING, inIVA
Josie Ballin, Press and PR Manager
Natasha Anderson, Marketing Manager

EXHIBITION IDENTITY
APFEL (A Practice For Everyday Life)

Alien Nation is a co-production by the Institute of
Contemporary Arts (ICA), London and the Institute
of International Visual Arts (inIVA), London.

We would like to direct our sincere thanks to all the
artists who have participated in *Alien Nation*: Laylah Ali,
Edgar Cleijne, Ellen Gallagher, David Huffman, Hew
Locke, Henna Nadeem, Kori Newkirk, Marepe, Yinka
Shonibare MBE, Eric Wesley, Mario Ybarra Jr. and
the late Hamad Butt

We would also like to thank our colleagues across
both institutions for their support of this exhibition:
ICA Mark Adams, Rosie Allerhand, Rob Bowman,
David Cox, Lee Curran, Ekow Eshun, James Harkin,
Donna Hay, Rose Hempton, Russell Herron,
Linda Huckstep, Teijinder Jouhal, Deirdre Kelly,
Claire Lloyd, Nick Luscombe, Guy Perricone,
Emma Pettit, Martha Pym, Emma Quinn, Duncan
Smith, Sarah Squire, Jennifer Thatcher, Ben Woodeson
inIVA Augustus Casely-Hayford, Kate Hall,
Obinna Nwosu, Linda Schofield

Furthermore we would like to thank the following
individuals who in various ways have helped to bring
this exhibition and publication together:

Alison Aitchison, Georg Bak, Julia Bell, Florian Berktold,
Isabel Bernheimer, Fred Bülow Ulson, Cristina Candeloro,
Kirsty Carter, Pamela Caserta, Kimberley Chandler,
Patrick Charpenel, Michael Clifton, Will Cunningham,
EVN Collection, Sam Forster, Stephen Friedman, Ulrike
Gast, Robert Graham, Enrique Guerrero, Cynthia
Gutierrez, Kathy Halbreich, Sophia Hoffmann Lambri,
Ralph Holmes, Geovana Ibarra, Gabriela Inui, Christina
Kennedy, Anton Kern, Judith Kerr, Nigel Kneale, David
Leister, Daniel and Mirella Levinas, Roni Lubliner, Heike
Maier-Rieper, Estefannia Krivov Meana, Fernando Meana
Green, Professor David A. Mellor, Ellen Miller, Janet
Moat, Jessica Morgan, Liza and Dr Arturo F. Mosquera,
Gregor Muir, Chris Mullen, Tony Nourmand, Nathalie
Obadia, Hans-Ulrich Obrist, Kelly O'Connor, Diletta
Ornaghi, Simon O'Sullivan, Linda Pace, Brian Palagallo,
Isabella Prata, Cesar and Mima Reyes, Larry Rinder,
Natasha Roje, Michael Roth, Roberto Rubalcava, Kirsten
Sampson, Heather Scanlan, Luisa Strina, Kana Sunayama,
Patricia Sweetow, Greg Tate, Emma Thomas, Hanne
Tonger-Erk, Valerio & Valerio, Lucio Zotti

In addition we would like to thank the following galleries
for their generous support:
Anton Kern Gallery, New York
Galeria Fortes Vilaça, São Paulo
Galeria Luisa Strina, São Paulo
Galerie Nathalie Obadia, Paris
Hales Gallery, London
Hauser & Wirth, Zürich London
Miller Block Gallery, Boston
Patricia Sweetow Gallery, San Francisco
The Project, New York
The Reel Poster Gallery, London
Stephen Friedman Gallery, London

We would also like to thank the individuals, institutions
and galleries that have so generously lent their works to
this exhibition:
Ivan Arcuschin, São Paulo
BBC Programme Acquisition
Ahmad Butt, London
Disaphol Chansiri, Bangkok
Steven D. Corkin, Boston
Peter Douglass, London
Damian Harland Collection, London
Hastings Collection, Los Angeles
Andy Johnson, London
Vincent Palser, London
Laura Skoler, New York
Daniel and Rena Sternberg, Glencoe, Illinois
Walker Art Center, Minneapolis
and those lenders who wish to remain anonymous.

Additional funding for *Alien Nation* has generously been
provided by Vicky Hughes and John Smith, London.

We sincerely thank The Reel Poster Gallery for the loan of
the film posters to the exhibition and images to the
publication, and for their invaluable advice over the course
of the project's organisation.

Finally we would like to thank Galeria Luisa Strina,
São Paulo as well as Patricia Sweetow Gallery, San
Francisco, for their individual support of the exhibition.

CO-PUBLISHED BY the Institute of Contemporary Arts (ICA), London and the Institute of International Visual Arts (inIVA), London and Hatje Cantz Verlag, Ostfildern, Germany on the occasion of the exhibition *Alien Nation*.

EDITORS
John Gill, Jens Hoffmann and Gilane Tawadros

COORDINATING EDITOR
Rebecca Wilson

COPY EDITOR
Linda Schofield

EDITORIAL SUPPORT
Claire Fitzsimmons and Cylena Simonds

PUBLICATION DESIGN
APFEL (A Practice for Everyday Life)

PRINTER
Dr Cantz'sche Druckerei, Ostfildern

TYPEFACES
Monotype Bodoni Ultra Bold and Ultra Bold Italic
Monotype Grotesque Regular and Italic
Monotype Sabon Regular, Italic and Semi Bold
Trade Gothic Bold Condensed No. 20 Regular and Oblique
Trade Gothic Bold No. 2
APFEL Split Alien (cover)
APFEL Quatermass (pp 1, 5, 7, 35–40, 67, 103–6)
APFEL Shattered Oblique (pp 9, 11, 101, 103)
APFEL Hoffmann Shudder (p.31)
APFEL Truth is out there... (p.33)
APFEL Pinched (pp 89, 119)
APFEL Space Odyssey (p.91)

PAPER
150 g/m² KIARA Gardamat 13, 170 g/m² Munken Lynx white

BINDING
Kunst–und Verlagsbuchbinderei GmbH, Leipzig

REPRODUCTIONS
Dr Cantz'sche Druckerei, Ostfildern

A catalogue record of this book is available from the British Library.

ISBN 1-899846-47-6 / 978-1-899846-47-4 (ICA/inIVA)
ISBN 978-3-7757-1944-5 (Hatje Cantz Verlag)

© 2006 ICA, inIVA and Hatje Cantz Verlag, Ostfildern

Texts © 2006 the authors
Images © the artists (unless stated otherwise)

The exhibition identity is an adaptation of the original US film poster, *Invasion of the Body Snatchers* (1956), by an unknown artist.

Institute of Contemporary Arts (ICA)
The Mall
London SW1Y 5AH, UK
Tel +44 (0)20 7930 3647 / Fax +44 (0)20 7873 0051
www.ica.org.uk
The ICA is a Registered Charity number 236848.
Financially assisted by The Arts Council of England.

Institute of International Visual Arts (inIVA)
6–8 Standard Place
Rivington Street
London EC2A 3BE, UK
Tel +44 (0)20 7729 9616 / Fax +44 (0)20 7729 9509
www.iniva.org
inIVA is a Registered Charity number 1031721.
Financially assisted by The Arts Council of England.

Hatje Cantz Verlag
Zeppelinstrasse 32
73760 Ostfildern, Germany
Tel +49 711 4405-200 / Fax +49 711 4405-220
www.hatjecantz.com

Hatje Cantz books are available internationally at selected bookstores and from the following distribution partners:
USA/North America: D.A.P., Distributed Art Publishers, New York, www.artbook.com
Australia: Tower Books, Frenchs Forest (Sydney), www.towerbooks.com.au
France: Interart, Paris, www.interart.fr
Belgium: Exhibitions International, Leuven, www.exhibitionsinternational.be
Switzerland: Scheidegger, Affoltern am Albis, www.ava.ch
For Asia, Japan, South America, and Africa, as well as for general questions, please contact Hatje Cantz directly at sales@hatjecantz.de, or visit our homepage at www.hatjecantz.com for further information.

Alien Nation is distributed in the UK by:
Cornerhouse Publications
70 Oxford Street
Manchester M1 5NH, England
Tel +44 (0)161 200 1503 / Fax +44 (0)161 200 1504
publications@cornerhouse.org
www.cornerhouse.org/books

Supported by   Media Sponsor

'WATCH THE SKIES EVERYWHERE... KEEP LOOKING... KEEP WATCHING THE SKIES.'

CHRISTIAN NYBY, DIR. *THE THING FROM ANOTHER WORLD* (RKO RADIO PICTURES/WINCHESTER FILMS, USA, 1951)